Praise for David Orr's *The Road Not Taken*

"The most satisfying part of Orr's fresh appraisal of *The Road Not Taken* is the reappraisal it can inspire in longtime Frost readers whose readings have frozen solid. The crossroads between the poet and the man is where Frost leaves his poems for us to discover, turning what seems like a fork in the road into a site of limitless potential, 'in which all decisions are equally likely.'"
—*The Boston Globe*

"[David Orr's] achievement in this shrewd and patient book lies in connecting Frost's deceptively folksy manner with the very things that make him matter." —*The Wall Street Journal*

"David Orr has written the best popular explanation to date of the most popular poem in American history."
—*The New York Times Book Review*

"[Orr] gives the poem a *very* close reading, line by line, almost word by word, and finds traps and contradictions everywhere. . . . This is the way all great poetry must be read—with close attention to each word and how they work with, and sometimes against, each other. . . . Frost's beloved and misunderstood poem will never seem the same." —*The Dallas Morning News*

"Orr blends theory, biography, psychology, science, and a healthy dose of pop culture into a frothy mix so fun, readers may forget they're learning something." —*Publishers Weekly*

"Orr presents a fresh, perceptive reading of the verse; places it in the context of Frost's life, other works, and public persona; and considers the meaning of choice in American culture. An illuminating voyage into the heart of Frost's poem and the American spirit." —*Kirkus Reviews*

"This entertaining book will appeal to poetry and American literature lovers, as well as to readers interested in the interweaving of art and culture." —*Library Journal*

"Orr is fascinated by why so many have read this poem so positively for so long, and what this fact reveals about the American soul."
—*The Christian Science Monitor*

ABOUT THE AUTHOR

David Orr is the poetry columnist for *The New York Times Book Review*. He is the winner of the Nona Balakian Prize from the National Book Critics Circle and the Editors Prize for Book Reviewing from *Poetry* magazine. His first book, *Beautiful & Pointless: A Guide to Modern Poetry*, was named one of the twenty best books of 2011 by the *Chicago Tribune*. He holds a BA from Princeton and a JD from Yale Law School, and he teaches at Cornell University.

DavidOrr.com

The Road
Not Taken

FINDING AMERICA IN THE POEM
EVERYONE LOVES AND
ALMOST EVERYONE GETS WRONG

DAVID ORR

PENGUIN BOOKS

PENGUIN BOOKS
An imprint of Penguin Random House LLC
375 Hudson Street
New York, New York 10014
penguin.com

First published in the United States of America by Penguin Press,
an imprint of Penguin Random House LLC, 2015
Published in Penguin Books 2016

THE LIBRARY OF CONGRESS HAS CATALOGED THE HARDCOVER EDITION AS FOLLOWS:
Names: Orr, David, 1974– author.
Title: The road not taken : finding America in the poem everyone loves and
almost everyone gets wrong / David Orr.
Description: New York, New York : Penguin Press, 2015.
Identifiers: LCCN 2015296204 | ISBN 9781594205835 (hc.) | ISBN 9780143109570 (pbk.)
Subjects: LCSH: Frost, Robert, 1874–1963. Road not taken.| Frost, Robert,
1874–1963—Criticism and interpretation.
Classification: LCC PS 3511.R94 Z8565 2015 | DDC 81/.52 —dc23

Designed by Gretchen Achilles

149062918

To Karen

Contents

Introduction

A young man hiking through a forest is abruptly confronted with a fork in the path. He pauses, his hands in his pockets, and looks back and forth between his options. As he hesitates, images from possible futures flicker past: the young man wading into the ocean, hitchhiking, riding a bus, kissing a beautiful woman, working, laughing, eating, running, weeping. The series resolves at last into a view of a different young man, with his thumb out on the side of a road. As a car slows to pick him up, we realize the driver is the original man from the crossroads, only now he's accompanied by a lovely woman and a child. The man smiles slightly, as if confident in the life he's chosen and happy to lend that confidence to a fellow traveler. As the car pulls away and the screen is lit with gold—for it's a commercial we've been watching—the emblem of the Ford Motor Company briefly appears.

The advertisement I've just described ran in New Zealand in 2008. And it is, in most respects, a normal piece of smartly assembled and quietly manipulative product promotion. But there is one very unusual aspect to this commercial. Here is what is read by a voice-over artist, in the distinctive vowels of New Zealand, as the young man ponders his choice:

Two roads diverged in a yellow wood,
And sorry I could not travel both
And be one traveler, long I stood
And looked down one as far as I could
To where it bent in the undergrowth;

Then took the other, as just as fair,
And having perhaps the better claim,
Because it was grassy and wanted wear;
Though as for that the passing there
Had worn them really about the same,

And both that morning equally lay
In leaves no step had trodden black.
Oh, I kept the first for another day!
Yet knowing how way leads on to way,
I doubted if I should ever come back.

I shall be telling this with a sigh
Somewhere ages and ages hence:

Two roads diverged in a wood, and I—
I took the one less traveled by,
And that has made all the difference.

It is, of course, "The Road Not Taken" by Robert Frost. In the commercial, this fact is never announced; the audience is expected to recognize the poem unaided. For any mass audience to recognize any poem is (to put it mildly) unusual. For an audience of car buyers in New Zealand to recognize a hundred-year-old poem from a country eight thousand miles away is something else entirely.

But this isn't just any poem. It's "The Road Not Taken," and it plays a unique role not simply in American literature, but in American culture—and in world culture as well. Its signature phrases have become so ubiquitous, so much a part of everything from coffee mugs to refrigerator magnets to graduation speeches, that it's almost possible to forget the poem is actually a poem. In addition to the Ford commercial, "The Road Not Taken" has been used in advertisements for Mentos, Nicorette, the multibillion-dollar insurance company AIG, and the job-search website Monster.com, which deployed the poem during Super Bowl XXXIV to great success. Its lines have been borrowed by musical performers including (among many others) Bruce Hornsby, Melissa Etheridge, George Strait, and Talib Kweli, and it's provided episode titles for more than a dozen television series, including *Taxi*, *The Twilight Zone*, and *Battlestar Galactica*, as well as lending its name to at least one video game, Spry Fox's *Road Not Taken* ("a roguelike puzzle game about surviving life's surprises"). As one might expect, the influence of "The Road Not Taken" is even greater on journalists and authors. Over the past thirty-five years alone, language from Frost's poem has appeared in nearly two thousand news stories worldwide, which yields a rate of more than once a week. In addition, "The Road Not Taken" appears as a title, subtitle, or chapter heading in more than four hundred books by authors other than Robert Frost, on subjects ranging from political theory to the impending zombie apocalypse. At least one of these was a massive international bestseller: M. Scott Peck's self-help book *The Road Less Traveled: A New Psychology of Love, Traditional Values and Spiritual Growth*, which was originally published in 1978 and has sold more than seven million copies in the United States and Canada.

Given the pervasiveness of Frost's lines, it should come as no surprise that the popularity of "The Road Not Taken" appears to exceed that of every other major twentieth-century American poem, including those often considered more central to the modern (and modernist) era. Admittedly, the popularity of poetry is difficult to judge. Poems that are attractive to educators may not be popular with readers, so the appearance of a given poem in anthologies and on syllabi doesn't necessarily reveal much. And book sales indicate more about the popularity of a particular poet than of any individual poem. But there are at least two reasons to think that "The Road Not Taken" is the most widely read and recalled American poem of the past century (and perhaps the adjective "American" could be discarded). The first is the Favorite Poem Project, which was devised by former poet laureate Robert Pinsky. Pinsky used his public role to ask Americans to submit their favorite poem in various forms; the clear favorite among more than eighteen thousand entries was "The Road Not Taken."

The second, more persuasive reason comes from Google. Until it was discontinued in late 2012, a tool called Google Insights for Search allowed anyone to see how frequently certain expressions were being searched by users worldwide over time and to compare expressions to one another. Google normalized the data to account for regional differences in population, converted it to a scale of 1 to 100, and displayed the results so that the relative differences in search volume would be obvious. Here is the result that Google provided when "The Road Not Taken" and "Frost" were compared with several of the best-known modern poems and their authors, all of which are often taught alongside Frost's work in college courses on American poetry of the first half of the twentieth century:

SEARCH TERMS	SCALED WORLDWIDE SEARCH VOLUME
"Road Not Taken" + "Frost"	48
"Waste Land" + "Eliot"	12
"Prufrock" + "Eliot"	12
"This Is Just to Say" + "Carlos Williams"	4
"Station of the Metro" + "Pound"	2

According to Google, then, "The Road Not Taken" was, as of mid-2012, at least four times as searched as the central text of the modernist era—*The Waste Land*—and at least twenty-four times as searched as the most anthologized poem by Ezra Pound. By comparison, this is even greater than the margin by which the term "college football" beats "archery" and "water polo." Given Frost's typically prickly relationships with almost all of his peers (he once described Ezra Pound as trying to become original by "imitating somebody that hasn't been imitated recently"), one can only imagine the pleasure this news would have brought him.

But as everyone knows, poetry itself isn't especially widely read, so perhaps being the most popular poem is like being the most widely requested salad at a steak house. How did "The Road Not Taken" fare against slightly tougher competition? Better than you might think:

SEARCH TERMS	SCALED WORLDWIDE SEARCH VOLUME
"Road Not Taken" + "Frost"	47
"Like a Rolling Stone" + "Dylan"	19
"Great Gatsby" + "Fitzgerald"	17
"Death of a Salesman" + "Miller"	14
"Psycho" + "Hitchcock"	14

The results here are even more impressive when you consider that "The Road Not Taken" is routinely misidentified as "The Road Less Traveled," thereby reducing the search volume under the poem's actual title. (For instance, a search for "frost's poem the road less traveled" produces more than two hundred thousand results, none of which would have been counted above.) Frost once claimed his goal as a poet was "to lodge a few poems where they will be hard to get rid of"; with "The Road Not Taken," he appears to have lodged his lines in granite. On a word-for-word basis, it may be the most popular piece of literature ever written by an American.

———

AND ALMOST EVERYONE gets it wrong. This is the most remarkable thing about "The Road Not Taken"—not its immense popularity (which is remarkable enough), but the fact that it is popular for what seem to be the wrong reasons. It's worth pausing here to underscore a truth so obvious that it is often taken for granted: Most widely celebrated artistic projects are known for being essentially what they purport to be. When we play "White Christmas" in December, we correctly assume that it's a song about memory and longing centered around the image of snow falling at Christmas. When we read Joyce's *Ulysses*, we correctly assume that it's a complex story about a journey around Dublin as filtered through many voices and styles. A cultural offering may be simple or complex, cooked or raw, but its audience nearly always knows what kind of dish is being served.

Frost's poem turns this expectation on its head. Most readers consider "The Road Not Taken" to be a paean to triumphant self-assertion ("I took the one less traveled by"), but the literal meaning of the poem's own lines seems completely at odds with this interpretation. The poem's speaker tells us he "shall be telling," at some point in the future, of how he took the road less traveled by, yet he has already admitted that the two paths "equally lay / In leaves" and "the passing there / Had worn them really about the same." So the road he will later call less traveled is actually the road *equally* traveled. The two roads are interchangeable.

According to this reading, then, the speaker will be claiming "ages and ages hence" that his decision made "all the difference" only because this is the kind of claim we make when we want to comfort or blame ourselves by assuming that our current position is the product of our own choices (as opposed to what was chosen for us, or allotted to us by chance). The poem isn't a salute to can-do individualism; it's a commentary on the self-deception we practice when constructing the story of our own lives. "The Road Not Taken" may be, as the critic Frank Lentricchia memorably put it, "the best example in all of American poetry of a wolf in sheep's clothing." But we could go further: It may be the best example in all of American *culture* of a wolf in sheep's clothing.

In this it strongly resembles its creator. Frost is the only major literary figure in American history with two distinct audiences, one of which regularly assumes that the other has been deceived. The first audience is relatively small and consists of poetry devotees, most of whom inhabit the art form's academic subculture. For these readers, Frost is a mainstay of syllabi and seminars, and a regular subject of scholarly articles (though he falls well short of inspiring the interest that Ezra Pound and Wallace Stevens enjoy). He's considered bleak, dark, complex, and manipulative; a genuine poet's poet, not a historical artifact like Longfellow or a folk balladeer like Carl Sandburg. While Frost isn't the most esteemed of the early-twentieth-century poets, very few dedicated poetry readers talk about him as if he wrote greeting card verse.

Then there is the other audience. This is the great mass of readers at all age levels who can conjure a few lines of "The Road Not Taken" and "Stopping by Woods on a Snowy Evening," and possibly "Mending Wall" or "Birches," and who think of Frost as quintessentially American in the way that amber waves of grain are quintessentially American. To these readers (or so the first audience often assumes), he isn't bleak or sardonic but rather a symbol of Yankee stoicism and countrified wisdom. This audience is large. Indeed, the search patterns of Google users indicate that, in terms of popularity, Frost's true peers aren't Pound or Stevens or Eliot, but rather figures like Pablo Picasso and Winston Churchill. Frost is not simply that rare bird, a popular poet; he is one of the best-known personages of the past hundred years in any cultural arena. In all of American history, the only writers who can match or surpass him are Mark Twain and Edgar Allan Poe, and the only poet in the history of English-language verse who commands more attention is William Shakespeare.

This level of recognition makes poetry readers uncomfortable. Poets, we assume, are not popular—at least after 1910 or so. If one becomes popular, then either he must be a second-tier talent catering to mass taste (as Sandburg is often thought to be) or there must be some kind of confusion or deception going on. The latter explanation is generally applied to Frost's celebrity. As Robert Lowell once put it,

"Robert Frost at midnight, the audience gone / to vapor, the great act laid on the shelf in mothballs." The "great act" is for "the audience" of ordinary readers, but his true admirers know better. He is really a wolf, we say, and it is only the sheep who are fooled. It's an explanation that Frost himself sometimes encouraged, much as he used to boast about the trickiness of "The Road Not Taken" in private correspondence. ("I'll bet not half a dozen people can tell who was hit and where he was hit by my Road Not Taken," he wrote to his friend Louis Untermeyer.) In this sense, the poem is emblematic. Just as millions of people know its language about the road "less traveled" without understanding what that language is actually saying, millions of people recognize its author without understanding what that author was actually doing.

But is this view of "The Road Not Taken" and its creator entirely accurate? Poems, after all, aren't arguments—they are to be interpreted, not proven, and that process of interpretation admits a range of possibilities, some supported by diction, some by tone, some by quirks of form and structure. Certainly it's wrong to say that "The Road Not Taken" is a straightforward and sentimental celebration of individualism: This interpretation is contradicted by the poem's own lines. Yet it's also not quite right to say that the poem is merely a knowing literary joke disguised as shopworn magazine verse that has somehow managed to fool millions of readers for a hundred years. A role too artfully assumed ceases to become a role and instead becomes a species of identity—an observation equally true of Robert Frost himself. One of Frost's greatest advocates, the scholar Richard Poirier, has written with regard to Frost's recognition among ordinary readers that "there is no point trying to explain the popularity away, as if it were a misconception prompted by a pose." By the same token, there is no point in trying to explain away the general misreadings of "The Road Not Taken," as if they were a mistake encouraged by a fraud. The poem both is and isn't about individualism, and it both is and isn't about rationalization. It isn't a wolf in sheep's clothing so much as a wolf that is somehow also a sheep, or a sheep that is also a wolf. It is a poem about the necessity of choosing that somehow, like its author, never makes a choice itself—that instead repeatedly returns us to the same enigmatic, leaf-shadowed crossroads.

———

IN THIS IT HAS a distinctly American flavor. American culture foregrounds the issue of choice itself, regardless of the results. Captain Ahab pursues the white whale not at the direction of a god or a king, but at the bidding of a choice inflated into mania. *The Adventures of Huckleberry Finn* is haunted by the fact that one of its main characters, Jim, is legally unable to choose—and yet does so anyway. *Casablanca* builds toward Rick's climactic choice while suggesting that even the personal decisions of a hard-drinking, heartbroken club owner are intertwined with political actions that affect millions. It's a way of thinking that flows naturally from the United States' earliest history. Here is John Adams writing to John Taylor in 1814:

> Liberty, according to my metaphysics, is an intellectual quality, an attribute that belongs not to fate nor chance. . . . The definition of it is a self-determining power in an intellectual agent. It implies thought and choice and power; it can elect between objects, indifferent in point of morality, neither morally good nor morally evil.

We want to believe that roads are taken (or not) by a "self-determining power" that can "elect between objects," as Adams puts it. Indeed, the nation's founding assertion that everyone is entitled to the "pursuit of happiness" assumes that a path can be chosen that will make that pursuit possible. Frost's lines simultaneously embody and undercut these ideas, but the ideas themselves are as American as action movies.

It's perhaps ironic, then, that "The Road Not Taken" was written in England and inspired by the indecisiveness of an

Englishman. That Englishman, the poet Edward Thomas, was, as Frost later put it, "the only brother I ever had." In 1912, when he was nearly forty years old, Frost traveled to Great Britain with his family in a last-ditch effort to improve his literary prospects; he was at that time almost completely unknown in the United States. He managed to get his work published in London, but it went mostly unnoticed until Thomas (then a prominent literary journalist) declared his second collection "one of the most revolutionary books of modern times." The men became good friends afterwards, and Thomas frequently visited Frost at his cottage in Gloucestershire. Throughout 1914, Frost and Thomas regularly took long walks in the woods and, according to Frost, these conversational rambles formed the basis for "The Road Not Taken." In the words of Lawrance Thompson, Frost's biographer:

> Repeatedly, while these two men had botanized in England together—Thomas leading the way through his favorite countryside in the hope of showing his American friend an extraordinary station of rare plants—these ventures had ended in self-reproachful sighs and regrets. Even the most successful of these walks failed to satisfy Thomas's fastidiousness. He blamed himself for having made the wrong choice of location and would sigh wistfully over the lovely spec-

imens he might have shown if only he had taken Frost
to a different place.

Frost sent the poem to Thomas soon after he finished it,
in early 1915. Britain was at war then, and Thomas had been
debating whether or not to enlist. He was troubled and con-
fused by the poem, and might even have read it as a goad.
Matthew Hollis argues for this possibility in *Now All Roads
Lead to France: The Last Years of Edward Thomas*:

> It pricked at his confidence. . . . The one man who un-
> derstood his indecisiveness the most astutely—in par-
> ticular, towards the war—appeared to be mocking
> him for it. . . . How free-spirited his friend seemed in
> comparison. This American who sailed for England
> on a long-shot, knowing no one and without a place to
> go, rode his literary fortunes and won his prize, then
> set sail again to make himself a new home. . . . "The
> Road Not Taken" did not send Thomas to war, but it
> was the last and pivotal moment in a sequence of events
> that had brought him to an irreversible decision.

Thomas joined the British army shortly thereafter. He was
killed two years later in the Battle of Arras, while lighting
his pipe.

So the confusion embedded in "The Road Not Taken" is

mirrored in the love and misunderstanding between its American author and his English friend. If this is an ironic parallel for such a thoroughly American poem, it's also a fitting one. The ideas that the poem holds in tension—the notion of choice, the possibility of self-deception—are concepts that define not just the United States, in all its ambiguity, but the responses that the United States inspires in and from citizens of other countries. There is the admirable self-reliance and the towering egoism; the emphasis on liberty and the thirst for control. There is the grandeur, and there is the hypocrisy. These contradictions come together in the idea of "self-determining power" that proved fatally compelling for Edward Thomas. This is why it's not so surprising, after all, to see "The Road Not Taken" used in a twenty-first-century Ford commercial in New Zealand. The iconic American poem, the iconic American brand—what better pairing to convince a Kiwi that his own "self-determining power" is central to the life he will lead and the choices he will make? And that this power would be enhanced by the purchase of a Taurus?

At the same time, of course, the advertisement itself is an attempt to undermine that power and replace it with the judgment of the advertiser and his client. It is, in one sense, a deception—as is "The Road Not Taken." Yet for all its trickery, no text from the past hundred years better captures the difficult essence of American experience, or more successfully translates that essence into a figure useful to people far beyond the borders of the United States. "The Road Not Taken" is a literary oddity and a philosophical puzzle, but more than anything else it's a way of framing the paradoxical and massively influential culture in which it both begins and ends.

The chapters that follow will examine these ideas through four windows. First, in "The Poet," I'll discuss the life of its author, Robert Frost, whose career parallels the reception of his least understood creation. Second, in "The Poem," I'll focus on "The Road Not Taken" itself: its origins, its teasing, contradictory lines, and its connections to Frost's later work. Finally, in "The Choice" and "The Chooser," I'll discuss the cultural and philosophical ramifications of Frost and his poem—a journey that should show how twenty short lines can change how we see the world, and how the world sees us.

The Poet

I began life wanting perfection and determined to have it.
I got so I ceased to expect it and could do without it.
Now I find I actually crave the flaws of human handiwork.
I gloat over imperfection. Look out for me. You as critic
and psychoanalyst will know how to do that. Nevertheless
I'm telling you something in a self conscious moment that
may throw light on every page of my writing for what it is
worth. I mean I am a bad bad man. But yours—R.F.

FROST TO BERNARD DEVOTO, *October 20, 1938*

To be perfectly frank with you I am one of the most notable
craftsmen of my time. That will transpire presently.

FROST TO JOHN T. BARTLETT, *July 4, 1913*

Before Robert Lee Frost was "Robert Frost," he was nobody. This is true of most major poets, in a sense. The reputation-building machinery of the poetry world is buried so deep in the trundling ocean of American culture as to be nearly invisible (and was similarly submerged even in Frost's day), so the larger reading public only rarely becomes accustomed to poets over a long, open, evaluative process. Rather, a poet who acquires any national reputation often seems to have appeared out of nowhere and all at once, like a whale breaching, as a thousand unseen currents come together. We choose our actors and popular musicians; we are presented with our poets.

But if a major poet's early career usually goes unremarked in the broader culture, his ambitions are rarely unknown among other poets and the people who read them. By the time he was thirty, T. S. Eliot had consorted with Alain-Fournier, been lectured to by Henri Bergson, befriended Conrad Aiken, allied himself with Ezra Pound, and become a project for Wyndham Lewis. By the time he was thirty-five, he was the controversial author of *The Waste Land*, an affiliate of the Bloomsbury group, and the editor of *The Egoist*, arguably the most significant literary periodical of the modernist era. (It published parts of *Ulysses*, among many other credits.) The average reader in 1923 would have had no idea who Eliot was, but the *un*-average reader—the elite reader—was another story.

Not so for Frost. At thirty-five, he was nobody even to the people to whom he might have been somebody. He'd published barely a dozen poems and a few stories in places like *The Eastern Poultryman* (yes, a journal for chicken farmers), and he was routinely rejected by literary editors in Boston and New York. It was a state of affairs that pricked his not inconsiderable ego. He'd been laboring at poetry since he graduated from high school, in 1892, and his devotion to that goal was challenged only by the iron relentlessness with which he had pursued his eventual wife, Elinor White. But it wasn't until 1912, when he was thirty-eight and his first book, *A Boy's Will*, was accepted by an English publisher, that Frost had any literary success to speak of.

Within four years, however, that book had sold more than twenty thousand copies in the United States—the equivalent of well over sixty thousand today—and Frost was abruptly among the country's best-known poets. There is no satisfying parallel in American literature for the rapidity of Frost's ascent, given the lateness of his first recognition; it's the kind of phenomenon for which the cliché "meteoric rise" is barely adequate. (By contrast, Wallace Stevens, who was born within five years of Frost, didn't arrive at his canonical position until age seventy, having seen his reputation rise for decades with the stately inevitability of a hot-air balloon.) Frost went almost immediately from being nobody to being not just somebody, but somebody whom other somebodies might want to court, or belittle, or appraise, or make pacts with. And this happened so quickly that the Robert Frost who had been alone with his family and his poetry for years vanished almost immediately behind a popular construction of "Robert Frost" that survives as a cultural touchstone to this day.

So deciding who—or what—Robert Frost actually was became an especially complex task. It became the kind of undertaking in which, as with "The Road Not Taken," it was possible to feel manipulated, or even tricked. This would turn out to matter both for Robert Frost the poet and for "Robert Frost" the national emblem.

———

BEFORE GOING FURTHER into the complications of Frost's biography, it's necessary to understand its basic outline and the rough shape of the work to which it's inevitably linked. Frost was born in 1874, in San Francisco, to a shy, deeply religious mother who is often described as "overprotective" and a journalist father who idolized Robert E. Lee as a boy (thus Frost's middle name), despite having been born in New England, and who supposedly carried around a Colt pistol, just in case anyone needed shooting. Frost had one sister, Jeanie, who struggled with physical infirmities and mental illness for most of her life.

After his father died from tuberculosis, at age thirty-six—leaving behind eight dollars—Frost moved with his mother and sister to Lawrence, Massachusetts, where his father's family lived. Frost was already eleven at the time, which means that a poet who would later be considered the personification of Yankee values actually spent the majority of his formative childhood years in a West Coast gold rush town. His mother taught school, and Frost quickly distinguished himself as a superb student and inordinately competitive athlete. He had a particular flair for Greek and Latin; as Jay Parini writes in *Robert Frost: A Life*, "His grades for 1888–89 included a 96 in Latin—something of a record for that era, when few students ever crossed the line into the 90s."

Frost graduated from high school as co-valedictorian, a fierce, sensitive, and somewhat pompous young man (as might be expected from such a precocious student) whose address was entitled "A Monument to After-Thought Unveiled." His companion at the podium was Elinor White, whom Frost fell in love with and became determined to marry. Though his feelings were reciprocated—they were secretly engaged shortly after graduation—Elinor went on to St. Lawrence College, in Canton, New York, while Frost entered Dartmouth with the help of a scholarship and financial assistance from his grandfather, a textile mill supervisor. (Throughout the first half of his life, Frost would repeatedly have to rely on his grandfather's largesse, a dependency that he came to resent.) Frost's time in New Hampshire was brief. He left school after only a few months, unhappy with his isolation and disappointed that Elinor didn't seem sufficiently agonized by his absence. He then returned to Lawrence, where he taught school, worked in one of the town's several mills, and did his best to get Elinor to marry him.

She said she wasn't ready yet, in part because she thought they should both complete their educations. So when the semester began, she went back to St. Lawrence and Frost immediately began to worry that she'd leave him for one of her fellow students. To forestall this, he had a booklet of five of his poems printed up and traveled to Canton to present it to Elinor, figuring that the gift would get her to change her mind about marriage, or at least get her to commit to him in a more satisfyingly definite way. Among the five poems was "My Butterfly," which Frost wrote in 1893, at age nineteen, and which is often taken to be the first poem in which his distinctive touch is evident. (Frost himself called it his "first real poem.") The conclusion is representative:

> Then when I was distraught
> And could not speak,
> Sidelong, full on my cheek,
> What should that reckless zephyr fling
> But the wild touch of thy dye-dusty wing!
>
> I found that wing broken to-day!
> For thou art dead, I said,
> And the strange birds say.
> I found it with the withered leaves
> Under the eaves.

Much of the poem is typical of the period, including the archaisms ("thy," "thou art") and a species of florid phrasing that seems clumsily poached from Percy Shelley ("reckless zephyr"). But there is a touch of the poet who would go on to write "After Apple-Picking" in the imagery and quiet formal dexterity of the concluding couplet: "I found it with the withered leaves / Under the eaves." The second line is, of course, literally under the first, allowing form to reinforce meaning, much as it does in the opening lines of Yeats's "A Prayer for My Daughter": "Once more the storm is howling, and half hid / Under this cradle-hood and coverlid / My child sleeps on." "My Butterfly" is a minor poem at best, but for a very young poet in the last decade of the nineteenth century, it's startlingly mature. Nonetheless, and perhaps not surprisingly, Elinor was unswayed by Frost's gift, and he returned to Lawrence in despair.

He then made the most peculiar trip of his life: a solitary, days-long journey to the Great Dismal Swamp, on the North Carolina–Virginia state line. It's not clear what Frost thought he would do there—he was evidently wearing shoes intended for streets, not bogs—but after stumbling around in the mud with turtles and water moccasins for about ten miles, he was picked up by some duck hunters and eventually made his way back to Lawrence. Parini tactfully calls this escapade a "self-dramatizing act of disappearance." For now, it's enough to say that when considering the various claims and counter-claims in the biographical disputes that I'll discuss shortly, one should bear in mind that Frost was the kind of man who, first, courts the woman he loves by printing up a volume of his own writing and, second, upon feeling himself rejected by that woman, travels over five hundred miles in order to walk into a swamp.

In the wake of this unusual episode, a chastened Frost regained his equilibrium, and the couple were finally married in December of 1895, notwithstanding the disapproval of Elinor's father, who considered Frost to be lazy, moody, and altogether a risk for his daughter. They had a son, Elliott, within a year. After an attempt to open a school with his mother foundered, Frost decided in 1897 to enter Harvard, where he hoped to study with one of his heroes, the philosopher William James. He easily passed the entrance exams (including a test on French, a language he didn't know) and enrolled, with support from his grandfather.

And again, it didn't last. Frost left Harvard in 1899, unhappy with the regimented nature of formal education and experiencing various physical ailments. He took up poultry farming and was having some modest success when Elliott contracted cholera, only two months after Frost's first daughter, Lesley, was born. The boy died, and Frost and Elinor fell into a depression that threatened to leave them destitute, if not homeless. (Their landlady sent them an eviction notice after visiting the property and finding it overrun with chickens.) Realizing the family would need to move, Elinor's mother began looking for a new home on their behalf. She found a promising-looking farm in Derry, New Hampshire, and with a loan from Frost's grandfather they relocated.

This would lead to one of the most condensed and fruitful periods of creativity in American poetry, if not American letters. Major poets generally have two or more strong periods over a span of decades—for instance, thirty-three years passed between the publication of Wallace Stevens's best-known poem, "The Snow Man," and the highly regarded poems gathered under the title *The Rock* in his *Collected Poems* of 1954. But Frost's body of work is dominated by his early efforts. "I might say the core of all my writing," Frost later wrote, "was probably the five free years I had there on the farm down the road from Derry Village." Indeed, over the next decade, Frost would write many of the poems that would appear in his first three books, including "The Oven Bird," "Hyla Brook," "Mowing," "The Death of the Hired Man," "The Wood-Pile," and "Putting in the Seed," and even poems that would appear in much later collections. ("Design" was written in this period but didn't show up in a book until twenty-five years later.) He also ran the Derry farm, albeit with a debatable degree of competence. Between 1902 and 1905 Frost and Elinor had two more girls—Marjorie and Irma—and a boy, Carol. (A sixth and final child, Elinor Bettina, was born in 1907 but lived only a few days.) When the growing family needed more money, Frost began teaching at Pinkerton Academy, a nearby school, where he acquired a reputation as an innovative if peculiar instructor.

But he was still almost completely unknown as a poet. So in 1912, at age thirty-eight, Frost decided on another major move—but this time, one that would be devoted entirely to the completion of a book of poems and the advancement of his literary career. He and Elinor flipped a coin between Canada and England, and England won. The couple's attitude toward this departure—an undertaking for which they had barely enough money, even with the sale of the farm— was surprisingly optimistic; their daughter Lesley later suggested to a friend that Frost and Elinor had wanted "a dramatic change of scene together," which is perhaps understandable, given the course their lives had followed to that point. In the fall of 1912, they set sail for Glasgow with their children and then made their way to London by train. They settled in Beaconsfield in a cottage called the Bungalow.

This proved to be the great turning point of Frost's life— the great road taken, you might say—for he almost immediately managed to place his first book, *A Boy's Will*, with an English publisher. And just in time. Frost and Elinor had been married for seventeen years, had moved countless times, had buried two children while raising another four, and had yet to make a stable living at farming or teaching. Frost was far from the young man who had walked into a swamp in a fit of desperation; his difficulties now had the weightier, less romantic character that comes with middle age and its subtle diminishments. "We poets in our youth begin in gladness," Wordsworth said. "But thereof come in the end despondency and madness." Frost's career doesn't quite turn this formula on its head, but his first successes came much further from the "gladness" of youth than the title *A Boy's Will* might lead readers to suppose. "We couldn't comprehend . . . ," wrote Lesley, "what resolve, what hope, what patience in waiting, had gone into that first book."

———

IT WAS SHORTLY AFTER the appearance of *A Boy's Will*—just as the glitter of eventual success was becoming evident—that Frost met the English critic Edward Thomas, who he would later claim inspired "The Road Not Taken." The two writers galvanized each other. Thomas was a widely admired book reviewer and essayist, but his own poetic ambitions had largely gone by the wayside as he churned out literary journalism in order to support three children. Frost urged him to take up poetry, which he did to great, if still undervalued, success. ("You are a poet or you are nothing," Frost wrote to Thomas in 1915, adding, in exactingly roundabout fashion, "But you are not psychologist enough to know that no one not come at in just the right way will ever recognize you.")

For his part, Thomas reviewed Frost's second collection, *North of Boston*, no fewer than three times, producing some of the sharpest early criticism of Frost. "These poems are revolutionary," he wrote in 1914, "because they lack the exaggeration of rhetoric, and even at first sight appear to lack the poetic intensity of which rhetoric is an imitation."

Thomas was right—and in particular, he was right to see Frost's achievement as antirhetorical, if not antipoetic. Frost's poetry, like Wordsworth's, takes as its launching point the common speech of ordinary people: The poet is "a man speaking to men," in Wordsworth's formulation. Frost himself is famous for declaring that poetry should be constructed from "sentence sounds," which he contrasted with the idea that poetry was "a matter of harmonized vowels and consonants." (He had in mind here the verse of Tennyson and Swinburne, in which it was common to find overpollinated lines like "The mellow ouzel fluted in the elm.") In Frost's view, the "sound of sense" to be found in great poetry was actually distinct from words as such, which can often express the opposite of their own semantic definitions.

Most of us understand this idea intuitively; we all know that the word "right" can be said in many ways to mean many different things, some of them very far from anything one would find in the dictionary entry for "right." ("I'm sure you've forgiven me by now." "Riiiight.") And of course, all poetry relies to an extent on the indeterminacy of language.

But Frost's writing seems not merely to rely on this indeterminacy, but to heighten and celebrate it. "All the fun's in how you say a thing," as he writes in "The Mountain"—and it's telling that the fun is in how you "say" a thing rather than how you "write" a thing. If Frost believed that poetry's strength lies in its ability to convey multiple meanings simultaneously, then he was equally committed to the idea that this ability depends on taking the rhythms of everyday speech as a model for poetic expression. We hear the essence of a poem, he believed, in the way that we hear "voices behind a door that cuts off the words."

It's a lovely image that at first seems almost modest: A Frost poem won't attempt to make a grand statement like *The Waste Land,* but merely to capture the homely contours of the human voice, forgoing elevated diction in favor of an effect that "principally has to do with tone," as he would put it in an interview. Yet the longer one thinks about it, the more this conception of poetry appears almost absurdly ambitious, because it aspires to a universality that (Frost implies) lies behind words themselves, somewhere in the meaning-making capabilities of intonation and syntax. It's one thing to say you're going to write poems that sound like people talking; it's quite another to say you're going to capture the essence of what it means to talk—and especially to talk from a position of barely masked personal extremity, as Frost's speakers often do.

And yet in the great work from the Derry years and the following interlude in England, that's very nearly what he managed. A typical Frost poem resists the idea put forward by John Stuart Mill that poetry is "overheard"—which is to say that poems stand in relation to readers the way intimacies stand in relation to eavesdroppers. Frost doesn't want to be overheard; he wants to be engaged. He wants to have, you might say, a conversation. (One of his lesser-known early poems is actually titled "A Time to Talk.") Or maybe it would be better to say the *appearance* of a conversation: Even Frost's most aggressively colloquial gestures lead to very unfamiliar territory, like hayrides that end on Mars. Consider "The Pasture," which begins *North of Boston*, and which Frost considered so central to his project that he used it again as a preface to his *Collected Poems*:

> *I'm going out to clean the pasture spring;*
> *I'll only stop to rake the leaves away*
> *(And wait to watch the water clear, I may):*
> *I sha'n't be gone long.—You come too.*

> *I'm going out to fetch the little calf*
> *That's standing by the mother. It's so young,*
> *It totters when she licks it with her tongue.*
> *I sha'n't be gone long.—You come too.*

The poem is an invitation, obviously, but an invitation to what? Well, to remove vegetation from a pasture spring and to "fetch" a newborn calf. Yet the first task is unnecessary—cows will happily drink from a pool covered in grass—and therefore seems motivated more by a personal desire to "watch the water clear" than by any practical purpose. The second task is a necessity in dairy farming, but not in the benign way many readers might assume. As critic Robert Bernard Hass notes, a dairy farmer "fetches" a calf in order to separate it from its mother, so that the farmer himself can ensure that the calf is properly raised to produce milk. Frost's project, the poem suggests, is to show that beauty and clarity are intertwined (waiting "to watch the water clear"), that this intertwining is a temporary luxury (the water will soon cloud over again), and that these moments occur against a backdrop that is anything but idyllic. The pasture, which is implicitly the poetry of Robert Frost, turns out to be a much more various and treacherous place than one might think.

But the most notable thing about the poem is how it addresses the reader: "You come too." It's an invitation, as I said, a tactic that is unusual enough in lyric poetry. But it's also an aggressively conspicuous invitation. When we see a quatrain whose first three lines rhyme *abb*, we're expecting the final line to rhyme with the first—*abba*—completing what's sometimes called an envelope stanza. (Just think how much more smoothly the first half of this poem would flow if its last line were something like "The oldest songs are easiest to sing.") But here the refrain breaks the anticipated pattern, throwing the words "You come too" into a relief that is heightened by their departure from the poem's previously iambic rhythm. Moreover, while the phrase "You come too" appears to be a suggestion (*Why don't you come too?*), it's equally possible to read it as a straightforward observation (*You are coming too*) or even a directive (*You* must *come too*). The reader necessarily "comes too" because the ostentatious ordinariness of the writing (which is predicated on our own patterns of speech) is what makes the pasture and "The Pasture" possible. The reader goes along—*we* go along—because we're simultaneously solicited, acknowledged, and compelled.

This is a lot of effort to expend on one's audience, and it runs strongly counter to the practice of Frost's most talented peers. For example, the opening remarks a reader finds on the first page of Eliot's *Prufrock and Other Observations* (1917) are six untranslated lines from Dante's *Inferno*, which is about as far from saying "You come too" as a poet can get. It's perhaps to be expected that Eliot and Frost remained unimpressed with each other until late in their lives. Frost, aggressive as always, mocked Eliot's pretensions for years ("I play euchre. He plays Eucharist"), and Eliot early on belittled Frost as "specializing in New England torpor." The tension between them was perhaps best outlined by Frost in a letter to John Bartlett in 1913 that addressed the ambitions of Eliot's great friend and promoter, Pound:

> There is a kind of success called "of esteem" and it butters no parsnips. It means a success with the critical few who are supposed to know. But really to arrive where I can stand on my legs as a poet and nothing else I must get outside that circle to the general reader who buys books in their thousands. . . . I want to be a poet for all sorts and kinds. I could never make a merit of being caviare to the crowd the way my quasi-friend Pound does. I want to reach out.

There are two points worth pausing over here. First, Frost's assumption that Pound and Eliot were interested in being "caviare" is the exaggerated version of an actual truth: Eliot wanted an audience for his poetry that was small, immensely learned, and (to take a quote of his slightly out of context) "very intelligent." If Frost wanted to reach out to the untrained many, Eliot wanted to pull back to the specialized few. And it is Eliot's ambition—with its concomitant assumption that poetry should not only *be* difficult but *look* difficult—that has given us the standard view of literary modernism as the art of self-conscious alienation. (The continuing dominance of that view is why it is still possible to see articles on Frost begin with sentences like these, from *Slate* in 2010: "Is Robert Frost . . . a modern poet? Or, in an academic refinement of the term, is he a Modernist?") Second, Frost's desire to be a poet "for all sorts and kinds" is perhaps not quite so generous and undesigning as it sounds. Addressing all sorts, after all, means failing to address any particular sort. Rather than seeking an audience, however small, that was fully equipped to understand his poetry, Frost pursued a multitude of audiences, each of which perceived only parts of him, and only from a certain angle. To hold these disparate groups together required the constant attentiveness of a veteran politician.

And Frost pays a price for that solicitousness, not the least of which is that some readers struggle to separate his poetry from the banalities of the day-to-day talk upon which it relies. It can be hard to see past the "New England torpor," as Eliot put it, to the canny artist. Yet even at his most colloquial, Frost is only rarely truly commonplace. Consider this passage from "A Servant to Servants" (the speaker is a woman who has spent time in an asylum, or so she says, and who now lives in domestic drudgery as the companion of an amiably dull farmer named Len):

> *It seems to me*
> *I can't express my feelings any more*
> *Than I can raise my voice or want to lift*

My hand (oh, I can lift it when I have to).
Did ever you feel so? I hope you never.
It's got so I don't even know for sure
Whether I am glad, sorry, or anything.
There's nothing but a voice-like left inside
That seems to tell me how I ought to feel,
And would feel if I wasn't all gone wrong.
You take the lake. I look and look at it.
I see it's a fair, pretty sheet of water.
I stand and make myself repeat out loud
The advantages it has, so long and narrow,
Like a deep piece of some old running river
Cut short off at both ends. It lies five miles
Straight away through the mountain notch
From the sink window where I wash the plates,
And all our storms come up toward the house,
Drawing the slow waves whiter and whiter and
*   whiter.*
It took my mind off doughnuts and soda biscuit
To step outdoors and take the water dazzle
A sunny morning, or take the rising wind
About my face and body and through my
*   wrapper,*
When a storm threatened from the Dragon's Den,
And a cold chill shivered across the lake.
I see it's a fair, pretty sheet of water, . . .

It's easy to see that Frost is borrowing from the rhythms and phrasings of day-to-day speech here. ("It's got so I don't even know for sure" sounds like something you might hear in a diner over a plate of corned beef hash.) But it's essential to remember that no one actually talks like this—which is to say, no one actually speaks in elegantly varied iambic pentameter; no one spontaneously produces metaphors (the lake is "Like a deep piece of some old running river / Cut short off at both ends") that serve the dual purpose of indicating the speaker's imaginative resourcefulness and reflecting her sense of becoming psychologically "cut off"; no one intentionally delimits that display of metaphoric fluency by repeating a banal line ("I see it's a fair, pretty sheet of water") in a way that not at all coincidentally mimics the way a lake's shores "cut short off at both ends" the deep water between them. Nobody talks like this; nobody has ever talked like this.

And that distinction, as Edward Thomas understood, was just as essential to Frost's success as the extent to which his poems really do seem like speech. Imitation, after all, isn't duplication. Frost didn't intend to replicate the patterns of ordinary conversation; he meant to mimic them—and, more important, to symbolize them. But to symbolize talking—as opposed to symbolizing, say, the fragmentary nature of Western culture circa 1915—meant a kind of self-conscious reduction: a pose that would "at first sight," as Thomas says, "appear to lack . . . poetic intensity." If Wordsworth posed as a man speaking to men, Frost wanted to seem like a man speaking *with* men, and the people with whom we imagine ourselves talking are rarely figures of revolutionary genius. Rather, like us, they're nothing special, or at any rate nothing out of the ordinary. One of the essential statements of Frost's ambition comes in a letter to William Stanley Braithwaite dated March 22, 1915:

> We must go out into the vernacular for tones that haven't been brought to book. We must write with the ear on the speaking voice. We must imagine the speaking voice. . . . I like the actuality of gossip, the intimacy of it. Say what you will effects of actuality and intimacy are the greatest aim an artist can have. The sense of intimacy gives the thrill of sincerity.

To seem perfectly ordinary and utterly unique at the same time: This was Frost's ambition. And as he rightly noted, it would encourage a "sense of intimacy" that would raise questions of sincerity. A "sense" of intimacy, after all, isn't actual intimacy, and the "thrill" of sincerity doesn't require that anyone was really sincere. They are "effects of actuality," in Frost's finely paradoxical phrase. They involve, one might say, a performance.

THE IDEA OF PERFORMANCE was central to Frost's poetry from the beginning, but after he returned to the United States in 1915, it began to be a factor in his public presence as well. Though he had considerable teaching experience, Frost was much less practiced at delivering his poems; in one of his first public "readings," in 1906, his poetry was actually read by a local minister because Frost was too tongue-tied to do it himself. But as he resettled his family in America—the Frosts purchased yet another farm, this time in Franconia, New Hampshire—Frost became increasingly adept at projecting the persona that would soon become his trademark. That persona was essentially an exaggerated version of the farmer he had once been, or nearly been. He began to take on the look and speech cadences of a rough-hewn, slightly salty Yankee man of the soil, dropping vowels into the back of his throat, spicing up his conversation with seemingly impromptu epigrams, and dressing as if he might at any moment do something intriguingly rustic. According to Louis Untermeyer, a literary critic who would become one of his most ardent supporters, Frost didn't lecture to his early audiences so much as he "talked, and as he grew more at ease with people, talked in what seemed a haphazard assortment of comments that developed into a shrewd commentary on poetry as it related to the state of the world."

Indeed, "he never 'recited' his poems, he 'said' them—sometimes, especially if they were new or short, he 'said' them twice. 'Would you like to hear me say that one again?' he would inquire." It took years for Frost to overcome the anxiety he felt before a reading, so the studied informality he cultivated upon his return home wasn't so much an affectation as a kind of armor.

That armor was necessary, because as the critic William Pritchard puts it, his arrival in New York from England was "accompanied by one piece of good fortune after another," and each piece seemed to call for more personal contact with the newly discovered farmer-poet Robert Frost. The day the family disembarked, Frost picked up a copy of *The New Republic*, only to find a favorable review of *North of Boston* written by Amy Lowell, the doyenne of American poetry. Soon he was being squired around Boston by the editor of *The Atlantic Monthly*, congratulated by professors at Harvard, written up in the *Boston Herald*, praised by the *Chicago Evening Post*, touted in *Harper's* by William Dean Howells (commonly referred to as "the Dean of American Letters"), interviewed by the *Boston Post*, and invited to give reading after reading after reading. Some of this attention was of Frost's own devising—for most of his life, he was an adroit if unsubtle behind-the-scenes manager of his own career. (A typical remark in a letter to Louis Untermeyer: "You make the point that there must be many poetical moods that haven't been reduced to poetry. Thanks most of all for seeing that and saying it in a review of [a] book by me.") But much of the attention given to Frost was simply the result of readers' being captivated by the "thrill of sincerity" they felt they found in his poetry.

The overlap with the developing Frost persona was almost total. Audiences liked Frost because they found his chatty, unpretentious performances "sincere" or "true" or "unaffected." The scholar Tyler Hoffman helpfully summarizes several such responses to Frost's readings over the years in "Frost and the Public Performance of Poetry":

Waco *Times-Herald* (Nov. 17, 1922): "The impression that Frost left with most of us was one of inexpressible gentleness, with humor and strength and whimsical sincerity."

Emma Mae Leonhard in the *English Journal* (February 1952): "Frost's reading is a truly conscientious performance, naturally and simply expressive, yet fully alive."

Henry Popkin in *Theatre Arts* (February 1952): ". . . what lifts Frost's performance out of the class of superior vaudeville is his homely, direct reading of his poetry, for which the rest of 'the act' provides an authentic but prosaic accompaniment."

Thomas Lask in the *New York Times* (December

16, 1956): "In his reading Mr. Frost, now past 80, makes his verse sound more homespun than it is. He is not afraid to slur a word, break a rhythm."

"His performance," Hoffman observes, "is not felt to be in any way dramatic or rhetorical. . . . It is felt rather to be brimming with sympathetic values, a true expression of an inner self (kindly, tolerant, compassionate)." He sounded like a witty, rural sage; he wrote like a witty, rural sage; there must be some part of him that *was* a witty, rural sage. Recall the way in which Edward Thomas describes Frost's poems: "They lack the exaggeration of rhetoric, and even at first sight appear to lack the poetic intensity of which rhetoric is an imitation." As the poetry and the image of the poet began to converge, the terms of praise converged as well: *natural*, *simple*, *sincere*, and, perhaps most telling, *authentic*.

That perception of authenticity became Frost's trademark, at least among general readers. This isn't to say that audiences failed to understand that Frost's writing and public readings were performances—as is clear from the above, the average journalist had no trouble linking a Frost lecture with "superior vaudeville." But they were performances that seemed tied to an ordinary person who understood other ordinary people, and the silvery thread of that connection was something that listeners and readers believed could be relied upon. He seemed not so much a poet as a man who happened to write poetry. Here, for example, is how *Time* magazine described Frost in March of 1923, in a short article titled "He Digs His Songs from the Soil of Vermont" (emphases mine):

> A poet of New England; but a poet first of all of the American character, Robert Frost is best known for his second volume of verse, *North of Boston*. Frost is *a farmer by nature*, that curious combination of dreamer and hardheaded Yankee, *more characteristic of tillers of the soil than of poets*. I like best to think of him sitting in the grass at the edge of a field back of his farmhouse in the Vermont hills. His large, nobly-formed head, with its loosely falling iron gray hair, bends slightly forward. He talks deliberately, softly, his somewhat piercing and remarkably blue eyes lighting now and then with mischievous humor.

"I like best to think of him sitting in the grass": You can't get much earthier than that. The Robert Frost described here is almost completely different from the complex, sensitive, vain, depressed, difficult man who wrote the actual poems, the one who had moved more than twenty times and who had really spent only about five years farming. Yet this version of "Robert Frost" can't be entirely separated from the other and was, for better or worse, essential to Frost's enormous success. Within nine years of his return to the United States, he had won his first Pulitzer Prize; he would go on to collect three more, making him the most awarded poet in American history. By the time his *Complete Poems* was issued, in 1949, his books had sold nearly 400,000 copies, which is equivalent to more than 750,000 today. That same year, *Time* featured him on its cover, echoing the magazine's previous endorsement:

> On the Vermont hills about Ripton, the red fires of autumn smoldered on the swamp maples and sumac, crept inward from branch tips, inched downward into the valley where the river brawls through the gorge. From a slab-wood cabin with its back set firmly against the valley's shoulder, cooking his own meals and dependent on no man, 76-year-old Poet Robert Frost last week faced the world. It is the vantage point he likes best.

Give me, one is tempted to say, a break. (The article goes on to mention Frost's "fierce blue eyes" twice.) And yet if this version of "Robert Frost" isn't right, neither is it entirely wrong—there is an odd twinning or doubling that allows the author of the article, while delivering a series of embarrassingly romantic comments about the poet ("the heavy, big-knuckled hand shaped to axhelve and pitchfork"), to make observations about the poetry that show an appreciation for its creator's decidedly *un*-romantic intentions: "The result was a deceptively artless poetry of common speech . . . partly serious when it seemed most irreverent, gently mocking when it seemed most grave." It's as if understanding Frost meant misunderstanding him at the same time.

This is perhaps unsurprising, considering the extent to which Frost became identified with America itself in his late career. If *Time* had considered him in 1923 to be "a poet first of all of the American character," by 1950 he had become "a native American voice unsurpassed by any American poet since Whitman." This elevation occurred even as his private life became bleaker and bleaker. In the span of only six years, his daughter Marjorie died after childbirth, Elinor died from a heart attack, and his son Carol committed suicide. "I expect to have to go depths below depths in thinking," he wrote to Bernard DeVoto in 1938, "before I catch myself and can say what I want to be while I last." Yet even the weight of these losses couldn't slow Frost's ascent. By the late 1950s, he was a recognized national figure whose autograph was routinely sought out even in the remote territory of East Middlebury, Vermont. (The Waybury Inn, where Frost used to have dinner, still maintains a Robert Frost Suite.) After his friend Sherman Adams, the former governor of New Hampshire, became a special assistant to Dwight Eisenhower, Frost met several times with the president, at one point giving him a book inscribed, "The strong are saying nothing until they see," a line from his similarly titled poem. (Eisenhower would later confide, "I like his maxim most of all.") When Frost was honored by the Poetry Society of America in 1958, Eisenhower provided a statement that practically wrapped Frost in the flag: "The sensitive and imaginative words of the poet contribute much to the spirit of a people. It is fortunate that our nation is blessed with Citizens like Robert Frost, who can express our innermost feelings and speak so clearly to us of our land and life."

But it was Frost's relationship with John F. Kennedy that transformed him from a merely famous writer into a national monument. Frost had supported Kennedy during his campaign against Nixon (it's a testament to Frost's unique status among poets that his goodwill mattered at all), and after Kennedy's victory, he was asked to read at the inauguration. He agreed, and the resulting two minutes are the closest American poetry has ever come to the sound, as Whitman puts it, of "a call in the midst of the crowd; / My own voice, orotund, sweeping, and final." You'd never guess this from the way the reading begins, though. As Frost approaches the podium, the first thing the modern viewer notices is how *old* he seems (he was eighty-six) and how vulnerable he looks in his enormous black coat, which seems as if it's been incompletely filled with satiny, overused pillows. Right away, he struggles. In the bright winter sun, he can't see the pages of the new poem he's written for the occasion—an awful piece, nearly doggerel—and he fumbles painfully through the first couple of lines, prompting Lyndon Johnson to offer his hat for shade. Frost refuses, with a joke, and then, only seconds before the episode would have collapsed into humiliation, puts the pages of the new composition aside and simply begins reciting "The Gift Outright" from memory.

> *The land was ours before we were the land's.*
> *She was our land more than a hundred years*
> *Before we were her people. . . .*

The granitic lines of the poem—which, like those of "The Road Not Taken," are both resonant and deceptive—rise irresistibly into the foreground. The moment is saved.

The next year, Kennedy would send Frost to Russia, where he would meet with Khrushchev. Though he would bungle the visit by announcing upon his return that the premier had described Americans as "too liberal to fight"—a remark invented by Frost, much to Kennedy's annoyance—he nonetheless had the distinction of being the only American poet ever to have spoken frankly with both of the midcentury's great leaders. "God wants us to contend," he told Khrushchev. When Frost died, the next year, his obituary, which appeared above the fold on the front page of the *New York Times*, ran more than 2,500 words and included this tribute from Kennedy: "There is a story that some years ago an interested mother wrote to a principal of a school, 'Don't teach my boy poetry, he's going to run for Congress.' I've never taken the view that the world of politics and the world of poetry are so far apart." They are united, Kennedy suggests, because their greatness depends on "courage"—it is what makes, as Frost might put it, "all the difference."

———

THAT, OF COURSE, would be a fine place for the story to end. But for a writer of Frost's density and vigor, the measurable life of the actual man is only a small part of the myth of the poet, which expands with the inexorability of kudzu through posthumous reevaluations of the work, posthumous discoveries of letters, diaries, and unpublished scraps, posthumous recollections of decades-old conversations, and, more than anything else, posthumous summaries of the life itself by biographers. As Auden puts it, with reference to Yeats, a great poet eventually becomes "his admirers," though people quoting Auden often forget that he adds, only four lines later, that Yeats will also be "punished under a foreign code of conscience." A dead writer often finds himself at the mercy of something other than friends.

And this is where the story of Robert Frost and "Robert Frost" becomes very strange indeed. Other major writers have had biographers who did them no favors, but Frost is the only significant poet to have an official biographer who actively despised him. In 1939, Lawrance Thompson was a Princeton professor who had long been, as he put it, "a Frost addict." (He had first met him in 1925, when he was an undergraduate at Wesleyan, and Frost subsequently supervised his dissertation at Columbia.) After another biographer died unexpectedly, Frost offered to let Thompson take the job in an exclusive capacity and with the poet's cooperation, so long as Thompson agreed to publish the book only after Frost's death. Thompson suggested that a closer friend might be more appropriate, but Frost rejected the suggestion on the grounds that such a person would be insufficiently objective—a decision so ironic that it's tempting to say it belongs in a Frost poem.

The pairing was a disaster. By the 1950s, Thompson had come to dislike Frost, Frost himself had become increasingly contemptuous of Thompson ("He's a charming man, but charm's not enough, is it?"), and both of them may well have become romantically involved with Frost's secretary, Kay Morrison, who became a constant companion in his later years. The poet was soon only half-jokingly asking friends to "save" him from his own biographer. They couldn't: A few years after Frost's death, Thompson issued a *Selected Letters* whose critical glosses made Frost look manipulative and petty at best ("Repeatedly throughout his life, RF indulged in a spoiled-child attitude toward any major crisis that thwarted his own wishes"). This was followed, over a roughly ten-year period, by three biographical volumes collectively weighing in at more than two thousand pages, the last of which had to be completed after Thompson's death by one of his graduate students.

The books are scathing toward Frost and, worse, are scathing without quite seeming to want to be so. Thompson wasn't a stupid man, nor did he want to write a bad biography; he understood that he wasn't fond of the poet and that he needed to guard against his own biases. Yet as the scholar Donald Sheehy has demonstrated by reviewing the biographer's source notes, Thompson became convinced that Frost was neurotic—that his personality, in fact, neatly dovetailed with a theory of neurosis developed by the psychoanalyst Karen Horney, whom Thompson had recently encountered— and under the cover of that diagnosis, his own antipathies bloomed. To show the general slant of the books, it's become customary among Frost critics simply to list some of the subheadings under "Frost, Robert Lee" in the index to any of Thompson's volumes: "Anti-Intellectual," "Baffler-Teaser-Deceiver," "Brute," "Charlatan," "Cowardice," "Enemies," "Hate," "Insanity," "Jealousy," "Murderer," "Rage," "Revenge," "Self-Centeredness," "Spoiled Child," and so on. As Thompson tells it, when Frost played baseball as a boy, it was because the sport permitted him to sling objects at other

THE ROAD NOT TAKEN

people's heads. When his daughter, distraught after the death of her mother, reproached him for selfishness, not only did this demonstrate a "habit of vindictiveness she had acquired from her father," but Frost also probably deserved the abuse (and Thompson hastens to suggest that Frost would, of course, soon seek out people who would reassure him that these accusations were more than he really should be asked to bear).

The effect of the publication of the Thompson biographical volumes, between 1966 and 1977, was twofold. First and most obviously, it encouraged contemporary literary critics to cast stones at Robert Frost the man in a way that would leave unmendable cracks in "Robert Frost" the legend, at least among the sort of readers who determine the fashionableness of poets. The essence of the criticism of Frost was that he was, in some sense, a fake: an abusive manipulator pretending to be a genial, if mischievous, elder statesman. In reviewing the final Thompson volume for the *New York Times Book Review* in 1977, for instance, David Bromwich described Frost in this way: "A more hateful human being cannot have lived who wrote words that moved other human beings to tears." He went on to pronounce the poet a "liar" and "terrifying." In this estimation, he was following in the footsteps of Helen Vendler, who had declared Frost to be a hypocritical "monster of egotism" who "left behind him a wake of destroyed human lives." Howard Moss, the poetry editor of *The New Yorker*, announced that Frost was a "mean-spirited megalomaniac." In a more nuanced and therefore even more damning piece for the *Saturday Review*, John W. Aldridge praised Thompson for resisting "the temptation to sensationalize those aspects of Frost's character that were reprehensible in the extreme," skipping nimbly over the fact that he had at his disposal only Thompson's account of "those aspects" in the first place. Claiming that "poetry . . . is an imaginary means of compensating for neurotic difficulty"—and presumably unaware that the biography was constructed around exactly this questionable notion—Aldridge went on to suggest that Frost was tempted "to murder," that he indulged in "the most abject fawning and flattery" and "exploited his family and friends to a degree that would seem contemptible." Collectively, these assaults created what Frost's increasingly embattled defenders called "the monster myth," a characterization that has proved durable enough to be referenced in the *New York Times* in January of 2014, more than half a century after the poet's death: "But now, a new scholarly work [*The Letters of Robert Frost*] may put an end to the 'monster myth,' as Frost scholars call it, once and for all."

The second effect of the Thompson biography was to underscore a fact about Frost that is as peculiar as it is unavoidable: Readers always seem to think he needs rescuing. And not just rescuing in the abstract, as from obscurity or obliv-

ion, but rescuing specifically from some other, less under-
standing or sympathetic person or group of people. In 1959,
Lionel Trilling caused a minor scandal when he spoke at
a celebration for Frost's birthday and declared him to be "a
terrifying poet"—which is true enough, in many ways, and
which Trilling plainly meant as a compliment. But the more
interesting part of Trilling's address was the way in which he
framed his analysis as a means of retrieving the "real" Frost
from the hoi polloi: "I have undertaken to say that a great
many of your admirers have not understood clearly what you
have been doing in your life in poetry." This, you might say,
is exactly what Frost's various readers have been busy assert-
ing to one another ever since. The Thompson volumes, for
example, were followed by numerous books and articles
intended not merely to add depth or further context to the
biographer's depiction of Frost but to directly rebut his por-
trayal. William Pritchard spends the first six pages of his
fine study *Frost: A Literary Life Reconsidered* analyzing
in detail the shortcomings of Thompson's style and approach.
Jay Parini's *Robert Frost: A Life*, the best recent Frost biog-
raphy, dwells extensively on Thompson's deficiencies ("Law-
rance Thompson, who wasted no opportunity to present
Frost as a monster . . ."), going so far as to include an after-
word that discusses the ways in which Frost "has generally
not been well served by his biographers." The posthumous
discussion of some writers resembles an amiable faculty

meeting, a conversation that gradually builds to achieve a resolution that is essentially stable. The posthumous discussion of Frost has been more like a battle—and there is no end in sight. When Joyce Carol Oates published a short story in 2013 that portrayed Frost as a depraved racist, she was promptly blasted by Frost scholars ("Oates's characterizations are so wrongheaded that they would be laughable were they not also malicious") and Frost's own grandchildren. To talk about Frost—even today, even in a book like this one—is to take sides.

BUT WHY? Certainly there are significant problems with the official biography; certainly Frost's unique celebrity has made him (for a poet) an unusually tempting target for hostile critics. But even so, why should the work and life of a writer dead for more than fifty years continue to inspire so much contention?

Here it's helpful to think a little about monsters—or, at any rate, about the word "monster." In summarizing Frost's biographical controversies, Pritchard writes that "the man who had been placed on a pedestal and worshipped in classrooms all over America was now seen—so the presumption went—for what he had really been all along: a monster in human form." Pritchard didn't seize on the word willfully:

THE ROAD NOT TAKEN

Not only had Vendler used it twice in her influential review of the Thompson biography, but variations on it had been deployed by several other writers. (Frost possessed "demonic vileness," according to novelist Harold Brodkey.) And as I said, the "monster myth" remains a journalistic catchphrase; typing "Robert Frost" and "monster" into Google will net you a quarter of a million results.

The word "monster" is a curious choice, not least because "fraud" or "hypocrite" or even plain old "jerk" would seem at first glance to be more applicable to the behavior at issue. After all, what is Frost accused of doing—or failing to do— that merits the word "monster"? The clearest statement of the charges appears in a review of the second volume of Thompson's biography by Vendler, who was particularly ap- palled by Frost's alleged mistreatment of his son Carol, who killed himself in 1940 (Vendler appears to be alone among Frost critics in arguing that Thompson was insufficiently hostile to the poet):

> Nevertheless, Thompson is capable of criminal bland-
> ness. He says placidly of Frost's son Carol: "There had
> never been any sustained affection between him and
> his father, and on many occasions each had antago-
> nized the other in ways that had built up lasting en-
> mities." Surely this is to apportion blame equally;
> Thompson forgets that Carol was a baby and Frost a

man when it all started. What is a father who has no "sustained affection" for his son but a monster?

One suspects that the reason that last sentence was written as a rhetorical question is that if it were rephrased as an assertion—"A father who has no 'sustained affection' for his son is a monster"—it would sound overheated. If being a difficult father made a man into a "monster," then goblin armies would lurk in every suburb in America. Frost may indeed have behaved badly toward his son, but Carol committed suicide at age thirty-eight, not age sixteen, and it seems remarkably ungenerous to Frost, to Carol, and to Carol's family to put the poet (then nearly seventy years old) at the center of that sad story.

So if critics aren't reaching for a word like "monster" in response to Frost's actual behavior, they must be attracted to it for some other reason. That reason, I suspect, has to do with the "thrill of sincerity" to be found in both Frost's poetry and in his public performances. Consider the relation between reader and speaker that is implied at the beginning of a well-known poem like "Birches":

When I see birches bend to left and right
Across the lines of straighter darker trees,
I like to think some boy's been swinging them.
But swinging doesn't bend them down to stay

As ice-storms do. Often you must have seen them
Loaded with ice a sunny winter morning
After a rain. . . .

"Often you must have seen them": We're explicitly included in the poem, and in a way that quietly suggests that the speaker should be taken as our representative—as "one of us." (*I have seen birches,* he says, *so you have probably seen them.*) Moreover, the easy casualness of the lines ("I like to think some boy's been swinging them") invites us to think of the poem as a conversation in which we're participating rather than, by contrast, a revelation we're being permitted to overhear. The effect is to establish a relation between speaker and reader that resembles the relationship between friendly neighbors more than it does the relationship between prophet and witness, or madman and bystander. (It's no coincidence that the word "neighbor" appears more than a dozen times in Frost's poetry, but not once in T. S. Eliot's.) Similar things could be said of Frost's public lectures, which strongly appealed to audiences' taste for the homespun intertwining of the everyday and the ordinary.

That appeal matters because the behavior of artists in their actual lives is judged more personally (and often more harshly) if an audience feels the behavior reflects on them, or in some way violates expectations encouraged by the work. Again, the example of a neighbor is instructive. Imagine that you have a neighbor with whom you've become not exactly close, but companionable. You and he have friendly exchanges on a regular basis, he lets your kids play in his yard, maybe he collects your mail if you go on a trip. You don't really know each other, but he seems like a generous, decent person, and you feel you have an understanding. Then one day, when looking after your neighbor's house while he's on vacation, you find a book lying open on his floor that has fallen off a shelf. It's a screed denying the Holocaust. A little Internet research reveals that in his spare time, your neighbor runs a conspiracy-theory website that traffics heavily in anti-Jewish slander. The website in no way advocates violence, and you've never seen your neighbor so much as scold his dog—you have no reason to think he's in any way a threat. But his behavior will probably preoccupy you now in a way that the behavior of some unknown, unnamed random person who runs a loathsome website never would.

The point is that while we judge people by their actions, that judgment is heavily colored by the terms of the relationship we believe has been extended to us. In Frost's case, the strangely intemperate response to his pedestrian, if unfortunate, flaws arises in part from the intimacy his work encourages. We thought we had an *understanding*. Remember that Frost says "effects of actuality and intimacy are the greatest aim an artist can have. The sense of intimacy gives the thrill of sincerity." An "effect" of actuality or intimacy is a symbol, not a pledge, but it's a testament to Frost's skill that he can blur that division so successfully.

———

YET IF IT'S NOT HARD to understand why a word as excessive as "monster" might be applied to Frost—however unfairly—that still fails to explain why "monster," in particular, has become the condemnation of choice. Here we have to look at the very carefully managed nature of the intimacy Frost encourages, and the equally carefully managed persona he developed. After all, other writers also have sought a "sense of intimacy" with readers, but not all intimacies are the same. The English poet Philip Larkin, for example, encouraged readers to find in his work the small, vulnerable part of themselves that feels put down or rejected by larger forces—the part that feels shame, that feels itself to be (unjustly, maybe) an object of disgust. ("They fuck you up, your mum and dad," begins his most famous poem.) The tactic is similar to Frost's methods, and it's therefore no coincidence that the publication of Larkin's biographical materials caused a scandal almost identical to Frost's. (To one reviewer, Larkin's letters were "a distressing and in many ways revolting compilation which imperfectly reveals and conceals the sewer under the national monument Larkin became.")

But Larkin isn't Frost. Larkin was widely perceived as

expressing a certain wry, enduring aspect of English charac-
ter, but it would have been nearly impossible to imagine him
reading at, for example, a royal wedding. The relationship a
reader enters into with Larkin's poetry seems more personal,
as if he were a slightly dissolute but much loved uncle who
embodies many of our own fears and doubts, and by doing so
redeems them. Frost was another matter entirely. As Trilling
noted in his infamous speech, by the middle of the century
Frost had become "virtually a symbol of America . . . not
unlike an articulate . . . Bald Eagle." Even Vendler calls him
"the Great Stone Face of American letters." Over and over,
Frost is described as if he were not merely a public figure,
but in some way public property. Upon his death, the *New
York Times* claimed that he "symbolize[d] the rough-hewn
individuality of the American creative spirit more than any
other man."

This was entirely in keeping with Frost's ambitions. "We
must imagine the speaking voice," said Frost—and the key to
this claim lies in its choice of article: not *a* speaking voice,
but *the* speaking voice. Frost's poetry works in a register we
should all recognize: It's the way of talking that allows us to
handle parent-teacher conferences or order food at drive-ins
or exchange information after a fender bender. It's a mutually
agreed-upon voice, a civic voice. It is the voice of the neighbor
next door, whom we may not know well but whom we rely
upon if the power fails. The intimacy of that voice—and it *is*

a kind of intimacy—suggests stability, normalcy, and authenticity. It's the sum of the small daily repetitions and reassurances that hold a community together: It belongs to no one in particular, but everyone in general.

And what lies outside the civitas, as the Romans might say? Everything that is chaotic, barbaric, and fraudulent—everything that is monstrous. Frost himself understood this quite well. Here he is writing to the *Amherst Student* on the subject of form, by which he means much more than poetic form:

> The artist, the poet might be expected to be the most aware of such assurance [of form]. But it is really everybody's sanity to feel it and live by it. Fortunately, too, no forms are more engrossing[,] gratifying, comforting, staying than those lesser ones we throw off, like vortex rings of smoke, all our individual enterprise and needing nobody's cooperation; a basket, a letter, a garden, a room, an idea, a picture, a poem. . . . The background is hugeness and confusion shading away from where we stand into black and utter chaos; and against the background any small man-made figure of order and concentration. What pleasanter than that this should be so? . . . To me any little form I assert upon it is velvet, as the saying is, and to be considered for how much more it is than nothing.

For Frost, the natural state of the world is lightless turmoil, and the small creations of isolated people are all that shines— for a moment—in that darkness. It's no surprise that when some readers felt that Frost's life might call into question the relationship his poetry seemed to offer, they reached for terms that signaled the opposite of that relationship. They looked away from Frost's forms and pointed at the shadow behind them. They pointed at its chaotic composition, at its refusal to adhere to patterns they thought it had adopted, at its bottomless appetite. They pointed at a monster.

———

FROST IS ALWAYS BEING RESCUED, always being reclaimed. He's like a disputed frontier, constantly contested, and this book is yet another stone thrown in that conflict. "No sweeter music can come to my ears," said Frost, "than the clash of arms over my dead body when I am down." But it's worth wondering whether the question ought not be what side a reader has taken with regard to Frost—benevolent or terrifying, modern poet or folk bard—but which choice a reader feels he has to confront. Because Frost trails contradictions like the wake from a battleship. Should we question his popularity, which seems so at odds with his massive erudition and technical accomplishment? Should we question his sincerity, which seems so dubious when one reads the scornful letters he wrote about his peers, and even his friends? Should we worry he is too much like us, or not enough?

Better, maybe, to think of Frost as a poet who asks us to ask these sorts of questions. It doesn't matter whether the "real" Frost is courtly or frightening, because the point is simply to make us wonder about "realness," about authenticity, about what it would mean to be truly sincere. In this sense, Frost is always placing us at the beginning of his most famous poem:

> Two roads diverged in a yellow wood,
> And sorry I could not travel both
> And be one traveler, long I stood . . .

The moment at the crossroads is the moment in which all decisions are equally likely. We haven't moved, we haven't chosen, we haven't sinned. And of course, one goes to the crossroads to meet the Devil, the angel who is also a monster. One goes to the crossroads to find America, the free land born in slavery. One goes to the crossroads to meet Robert Frost.

The Poem

_____

My poems—I should suppose everybody's poems—are all
set to trip the reader head foremost into the boundless.
Ever since infancy I have had the habit of leaving my
blocks carts chairs and such like ordinaries where people
would be pretty sure to fall forward over them in the dark.
Forward, you understand, and *in the dark.*

FROST TO LEONIDAS W. PAYNE JR., *November 1, 1927*

The Road Not Taken" has confused audiences literally from the beginning. In the spring of 1915, Frost sent an envelope to Edward Thomas that contained only one item: a draft of "The Road Not Taken," under the title "Two Roads." According to Lawrance Thompson, Frost had been inspired to write the poem by Thomas's habit of regretting whatever path the pair took during their long walks in the countryside— an impulse that Frost equated with the romantic predisposition for "crying over what might have been." Frost, Thompson writes, believed that his friend "would take the poem as a gentle joke and would protest, 'Stop teasing me.'"

That wasn't what occurred. Instead, Thomas sent Frost an admiring note in which it was evident that he had assumed the poem's speaker was a version of Frost, and that the final line was meant to be read as generations of high school valedictorians have assumed. The sequence of their correspondence on the poem is a miniature version of the confusion "The Road Not Taken" would provoke in millions of subsequent readers:

(1) Frost sends the poem to Thomas, with no clarifying text, in March or April of 1915.

(2) Thomas responds shortly thereafter in a letter now evidently lost but referred to in later correspondence, calling the poem "staggering" but missing Frost's intention.

(3) Frost responds in a letter (the date is unclear) to ask Thomas for further comment on the poem, hoping to hear that Thomas understood that it was at least in part addressing his own behavior.

(4) Thomas responds in a letter dated June 13, 1915, explaining that "the simple words and unemphatic rhythms were not such as I was accustomed to expect great things, things I like, from. It staggered me to think that perhaps I had always

missed what made poetry poetry." It's still clear that Thomas doesn't quite understand the poem's stance or Frost's "joke" at his expense.

(5) Frost writes back on June 26, 1915: "Methinks thou strikest too hard in so small a matter. A tap would have settled my poem. I wonder if it was because you were trying too much out of regard for me that you failed to see that the sigh [in line 16] was a mock sigh, hypo-critical for the fun of the thing. I dont suppose I was ever sorry for anything I ever did except by assumption to see how it would feel."

(6) Thomas responds on July 11, 1915: "You have got me again over the Path not taken & no mistake . . . I doubt if you can get anybody to see the fun of the thing without showing them & advising them which kind of laugh they are to turn on."

Edward Thomas was one of the keenest literary thinkers of his time, and the poem was meant to capture aspects of his own personality and past. Yet even Thomas needed explicit instructions—indeed, six entire letters—in order to appreciate the series of double games played in "The Road Not Taken." That misperception galled Frost. As Thompson writes, Frost "could never bear to tell the truth about the failure of this lyric to perform as he intended it. Instead, he frequently told an idealized version of the story" in which, for instance, Thomas said, "What are you trying to do with me?" or "What are you doing with my character?" One can understand Frost's unhappiness, considering that the poem was misunderstood by one of his own early biographers, Elizabeth Shepley Sergeant ("Thomas, all his life, lived on the deeply isolated, lonely and subjective 'way less travelled by' which Frost had chosen in youth"), and also by the eminent poet-critic Robert Graves, who came to the somewhat baffling conclusion that the poem had to do with Frost's "agonized decision" not to enlist in the British army. (There is no evidence that Frost ever contemplated doing so, in agony or otherwise.) Lyrics that are especially lucid and accessible are sometimes described as "critic-proof"; "The Road Not Taken"—at least in its first few decades—came close to being reader-proof.

———

THE DIFFICULTY WITH "The Road Not Taken" starts, appropriately enough, with its title. Recall the poem's conclusion: "Two roads diverged in a wood, and I— / I took the one less traveled by, / And that has made all the difference." These are not only the poem's best-known lines, but the ones that capture what most readers take to be its central image: a lonely path that we take at great risk, possibly for great reward. So vivid is that image that many readers simply assume that the poem is called "The Road Less Traveled." Search-engine data indicates that searches for "Frost" and "Road Less Traveled" (or "Travelled") are extremely common, and even accomplished critics routinely refer to the poem by its most famous line. For example, in an otherwise penetrating essay on Frost's ability to say two things at once, Kathryn Schulz, the book reviewer for *New York* magazine, mistakenly calls the poem "The Road Less Traveled" and then, in an irony Frost might have savored, describes it as "not-very-Frosty."

Because the poem *isn't* "The Road Less Traveled." It's "The Road Not Taken." And the road not taken, of course, is the road one didn't take—which means that the title passes over the "less traveled" road the speaker claims to have followed in order to foreground the road he never tried. The title isn't about what he did; it's about what he didn't do. Or is it? The more one thinks about it, the more difficult it becomes to be sure who is doing what and why. As the scholar Mark Richardson puts it:

> Which road, after all, is the road "not taken"? Is it the one the speaker takes, which, according to his last description of it, is "less travelled"—that is to say, not taken *by others*? Or does the title refer to the suppos-

edly better-travelled road that the speaker himself fails to take? Precisely *who* is *not* doing the taking?

We know that Frost originally titled the poem "Two Roads," so renaming it "The Road Not Taken" was a matter of deliberation, not whim. Frost wanted readers to ask the questions Richardson asks.

More than that, he wanted to juxtapose two visions—two possible poems, you might say—at the very beginning of his lyric. The first is the poem that readers think of as "The Road Less Traveled," in which the speaker is quietly congratulating himself for taking an uncommon path (that is, a path not taken by others). The second is the parodic poem that Frost himself claimed to have originally had in mind, in which the dominant tone is one of self-dramatizing regret (over the path not taken by the speaker). These two potential poems revolve around each other, separating and overlapping like clouds in a way that leaves neither reading perfectly visible. If this is what Frost meant to do, then it's reasonable to wonder if, as Thomas suggested, he may have outsmarted himself in addition to casual readers.

But this depends on what you think "The Road Not Taken" is trying to say. If you believe the poem is meant to take a position on will, agency, the nature of choice, and so forth—as the majority of readers have assumed—then it can seem unsatisfying (at best "a kind of joke," as Schulz puts it).

But if you think of the poem not as stating various viewpoints but rather as performing them, setting them beside and against one another, then a very different reading emerges. Here it's helpful, as is so often the case, to call upon a nineteenth-century logician. In *The Elements of Logic*, Richard Whately describes the fallacy of substitution like so:

> Two distinct objects may, by being dexterously presented, again and again in quick succession, to the mind of a cursory reader, be so associated together *in his thoughts*, as to be conceived capable . . . of being *actually* combined in practice. The fallacious belief thus induced bears a striking resemblance to the optical illusion effected by that ingenious and philosophical toy called the Thaumatrope; in which two objects painted on opposite sides of a card,—for instance a man, and a horse,—a bird, and a cage,—are, by a quick rotatory motion, made to impress the eye in combination, so as to form one picture, of the man on the horse's back, the bird in the cage, etc.

What is fallacious in an argument can be mesmerizing in a poem. "The Road Not Taken" acts as a kind of thaumatrope, rotating its two opposed visions so that they seem at times to merge. And that merging is produced not by a careful blending of the two—a union—but by "rapid and frequent transition," as Whately puts it. The title itself is a small but potent engine that drives us first toward one untaken road and then immediately back to the other, producing a vision in which we appear somehow on both roads, or neither.

———

THAT SENSE OF MOVEMENT is critical to the manner in which the poem unfolds. We are continually being "reset" as we move through the stanzas, with the poem pivoting from one reading to the other so quickly that it's easy to miss the transitions. This is true even of its first line. Here's how the poem begins:

> Two roads diverged in a yellow wood,
> And sorry I could not travel both
> And be one traveler, long I stood
> And looked down one as far as I could
> To where it bent in the undergrowth . . .

The most significant word in the stanza—and perhaps the most overlooked yet essential word in the poem—is "roads." Frost could, after all, have said two "paths" or "trails" or "tracks" and conveyed nearly the same concept. Yet, as the scholar George Monteiro observes:

Frost seems to have deliberately chosen the word "roads." . . . In fact, on one occasion when he was asked to recite his famous poem, "Two paths diverged in a yellow wood," Frost reacted with such feeling— "Two *roads*!"—that the transcription of his reply made it necessary both to italicize the word "roads" and to follow it with an exclamation point. Frost recited the poem all right, but, as his friend remembered, "he didn't let me get away with 'two paths!'"

What is gained by "roads"? Primarily two things. First, a road, unlike a path, is necessarily man-made. Dante may have found his life similarly changed "in a dark wood," but Frost takes things a step further by placing his speaker in a setting that combines the natural world with civilization— yes, the traveler is alone in a forest, but whichever way he goes, he follows a course built by other people, one that will be taken, in turn, by still other people long after he has passed. The act of choosing may be solitary, but the context in which it occurs is not. Second, as Wendell Berry puts it, a path differs from a road in that it "obeys the natural contours; such obstacles as it meets it goes around." A road is an assertion of will, not an accommodation. So the speaker's decision, when it comes, whatever it is, will be an act of will that can occur only within the bounds of another such act—a way of looking at the world that simultaneously undercuts and strengthens the idea of individual choice.

This doubled effect continues in the poem's second and third lines, which summarize the dilemma around which "The Road Not Taken" is constructed: "And sorry I could not travel both / And be one traveler . . ." Frost often likes to use repetition and its cousin, redundancy, to suggest the complex contours of seemingly simple concepts. In this case, we have what seems like the most straightforward proposition imaginable: If a road forks, a single person can't "travel both" branches. But the concept is oddly extended to include the observation that one can't "travel both" and "be one traveler," which seems superfluous. After all, Frost might more easily and obviously have written the stanza like so (emphasis mine):

> *Two roads diverged in a yellow wood,*
> *And sorry I could not travel both*
> To where they ended, *long I stood*
> *And looked down one as far as I could*
> *To where it bent in the undergrowth . . .*

What, then, is the difference between saying one can't "travel both" roads and saying one can't "travel both / And be one traveler"? And why does Frost think that difference worth preserving? One way to address these questions is to think about what the speaker is actually suggesting he's "sorry" about. He isn't, for instance, sorry that he won't see what's at the end of each road. (If he were, it would make more sense to use the modified version above.) Rather, he's sorry he lacks the *capability* to see what's at the end of each road—he's objecting not to the outcome of the principle that you can't be two places at once, but to the principle itself. He's resisting the idea of a universe in which his selfhood is limited, in part by being subject to choices. (Compare this to the case of a person who regrets that he can't travel through time not because he wishes he could, say, attend the premiere of *Hamlet*, but simply because he wants to experience time travel.)

This assumes, of course, that the speaker regrets that he can't travel both roads simultaneously. But what if he instead means that it would be impossible to "travel both / And be one traveler" even if he returned later to take the second road? As Robert Faggen puts it, the suggestion here is that "experience alters the traveler": The act of choosing changes the person making the choice. This point will be quietly reinforced two stanzas later, when the speaker says that "knowing how way leads on to way, / I doubted if I should ever come back"—the doubt is not only that he might return again to the same physical spot, but that he could return to the crossroads as the same person, the same "I," who left it. This reading of the poem is subtly different from, and bolder than, the idea that existence is merely subject to the need to make decisions. If we can't persist unchanged through any one choice, then every choice becomes a matter of existential significance—after all, we aren't merely deciding to go left or right; we're transforming our very selves. At the same time, however, if each choice changes the self, then at some point the "self" in question becomes nothing more than a series of accumulated actions, many of them extremely minor. Frost's peculiar addition—"And be one traveler"—consequently both elevates and reduces the idea of the chooser while at the same time both elevating and reducing the choice. The thaumatrope spins, the roads blur and merge.

————

THIS IS ONLY the first stanza of "The Road Not Taken," and already its lines seem papered over with potential interpretations, some more plausible than others, but none of which can be discarded. One can see why Thomas said he found the poem "staggering." But then Frost takes things a step further. Having sketched the speaker and his potential choice in all their entangled ambiguity, he undermines the idea that there is really a choice to be made at all:

> Then took the other, as just as fair,
> And having perhaps the better claim,
> Because it was grassy and wanted wear;

Though as for that the passing there
Had worn them really about the same,

And both that morning equally lay
In leaves no step had trodden black.

The speaker wants to see the paths as different (one has "perhaps the better claim") but admits that the distinctions, if they even exist, are minute ("the passing there / Had worn them really about the same"). The sameness of the roads will later be revised in the story the speaker says he'll be telling "ages and ages hence"—as he famously observes, he'll *claim* to have taken "the one less traveled by."

Two things are worth pausing over in these stanzas. First, why is the physical appearance of the roads mentioned in the first place? We typically worry more about where roads go than what they look like. (Here again it's worth contrasting "road" with "path" or "trail," neither of which implies a destination as strongly as "road.") So if all Frost intended was to parody a kind of romantic longing for missed opportunities, wouldn't it be more effective to imply that the roads reached the same location? As in:

Then took the other, as just as fair,
And making perhaps the better case,
Because it seemed to lead elsewhere,

Though at day's end each traveler there
Would finish in the selfsame place.

Second, if you're determined to make the appearance of the roads the central issue, why make that appearance solely a function of how much travel each road had received? Why not talk about how one road was sunnier or wider or stonier or steeper? "I took the one less traveled by" is often assumed to mean "I took the more difficult road," but this isn't necessarily true in either a literal or metaphorical sense. In scenic areas, after all, the less traveled paths are usually the least interesting and challenging (think of an emergency-vehicle access road in a state park), and if we imagine "roads" as referring to "life choices," the array of decisions that are "less traveled" yet both easy and potentially harmful is nearly endless (drug abuse, tax evasion, and so on). So if the idea was to suggest that the speaker wants to perceive his chosen road as not just lonely, but demanding, why not make a more direct statement that would lead to a more direct conclusion, like:

Two roads diverged in a wood, and I—
I took the one that dared me to try.

These lines are bad, admittedly, but not much worse at first glance than the poem's actual concluding lines, which involve the addition of an apparently superfluous preposition—

"by"—that is almost always omitted when the poem's crowning statement is invoked. (There's a reason M. Scott Peck's bestseller is called *The Road Less Traveled* rather than *The Road Less Traveled By.*)

So what's going on here? Again, it's helpful to imagine "The Road Not Taken" as consisting of alternate glimpses of two unwritten poems, one the common misconception, the other the parody Frost sometimes claimed to have intended. Every time the poem threatens to clarify as one or the other, it resists, moving instead into an uncertain in-between space in which both are faintly apparent, like overlapping ghosts. This is relatively easy to see with respect to the "naive" reading of "The Road Not Taken" as a hymn to stoic individualism. Had Frost wanted to write that poem, it would indeed have been titled "The Road Less Traveled," and it might have gone something like this:

Two roads diverged in a yellow wood,
And sorry I could not travel both
To where they ended, long I stood
And looked down one as far as I could
To where it bent in the undergrowth;

Then took the other, as just as fair,
And posing perhaps the greater test,
Because it was narrow and wanted wear,

Rising so steeply into thinning air
That a man would struggle just to rest,

While the other offered room to play
Or stand at ease along the track.
I took the lonelier road that day,
And knowing how way leads on to way,
I doubted if I should ever come back.

I shall be telling this with a sigh
Somewhere ages and ages hence:
Two roads diverged in a wood, and I—
I took the one that dared me to try,
And that has made all the difference.

I make no claims for the elegance of this version, but it does have all the elements generally attributed to the actual "Road Not Taken": an emphasis on solitary challenge, a tone of weary yet quietly confident resignation (what a skeptic would call self-congratulation), and a plain choice between obviously different options. It would have been easy for Frost to write this poem.

Yet that's not what he did. But neither did he write the parody that "The Road Not Taken" is widely considered to be among more sophisticated readers (or at least more careful readers). Frost had a barbed, nimble wit, and he would have had no trouble skewering romantic dithering more

pointedly if that was all he had in mind. Such a poem might
have been called "Two Roads" and gone like so:

Two roads diverged in a yellow wood,
And sorry I could not travel both
To where they ended, long I stood
And looked down one as far as I could
To where it bent in the undergrowth;

Then took the other, as just as fair,
And making perhaps the better case,
Because it seemed to lead elsewhere,
Though at day's end each traveler there
Would finish in the selfsame place,

For both, I learned, were arms that lay
Around the wood and met in one track.
And whichever one I took that day
Would lead itself to the other way
And send me forward to take me back.

Still, I shall be claiming with a sigh
Somewhere ages and ages hence:
Two roads diverged in a wood, and I—
I took the one on the left-hand side,
And that has made all the difference.

One of the essential elements of a parody is that it is recognized as such: A parody that is too obscure has failed its basic purpose. In "The Road Not Taken," Frost passes up several opportunities to make his "joke" more explicit, most notably by failing to give the roads a shared destination rather than simply a similar condition of wear. (And even that similarity is qualified, because it depends on the speaker's perception, not his actual knowledge—after all, having failed to take the first road, he can't be sure how traveled it is or isn't, beyond his immediate line of sight.) The usual interpretation of "The Road Not Taken" is almost certainly wrong, but the idea that the poem is a parody doesn't seem exactly right, either.

———

AND THIS BRINGS US to the final stanza—more particularly, it brings us to one of the most carefully placed words in this delicately balanced arrangement. That word is "sigh":

I shall be telling this with a sigh
Somewhere ages and ages hence . . .

Frost mentions the sigh several times in his remarks about "The Road Not Taken," and while those comments are often oblique, it's evident that he considered the word "sigh" essential to understanding the poem. It is "a mock sigh, hypocritical for the fun of the thing," he told Edward Thomas in 1915. It is "absolutely saving," he told an audience at the Bread Loaf Conference half a century later. According to Lawrance Thompson, he would sometimes claim during public readings that a young girl had asked him about the sigh, and that he considered this a very good question—an anecdote that (in Thompson's view) was meant to encourage the audience to appreciate the poem's intricacy.

But why would it? After all, a sigh fits both of the usual readings of the poem, and therefore doesn't seem likely to make either of them more interesting. If we give the poem its popular, naive interpretation, then the sigh is one of tired yet self-assured acceptance bordering on satisfaction: The speaker has taken the hard road, faced obstacles, lost things along the way, regrets, he's had a few—and yet he's ended up in a better, stronger place. It's a sigh of hard-won maturity or tedious faux humility, depending on how you look at it. By contrast, if we think of the poem as an ironic commentary on romantic self-absorption, then the sigh signals straightforward regret: The speaker is genuinely troubled by the consequences of every small choice he makes, and his preoccupation with his own decisions renders him slightly ridiculous.

But neither of these explanations for the sigh seems especially obscure, let alone "absolutely saving." Perhaps that's because both of them glide past a key point: The sigh hasn't yet occurred. Recall the final stanza:

I shall be telling this with a sigh
Somewhere ages and ages hence:
Two roads diverged in a wood, and I—
I took the one less traveled by,
And that has made all the difference.

The speaker isn't "telling this with a sigh" now; he's say-ing that he'll be sighing "ages and ages hence." He knows himself well enough—or thinks he does—to predict how he'll feel about the consequences of his choice in the future. But if he actually knows himself this well, then it's reason-able to ask whether he would, in fact, behave in the way he's suggesting. Which is to say that the speaker isn't necessarily the kind of person who sighs while explaining that many years ago he took the less traveled road; rather, he's the kind of person who *thinks* he would sigh while telling us this story. He's assuming that he'll do something that will strike others as either self-congratulatory or paralyzingly anxious.

It's a small difference, but as with so many small differ-ences in "The Road Not Taken," it matters a great deal. Be-cause it allows us to feel affectionate compassion toward the speaker, whom it's now possible to view less as a boaster or a neurotic than as a person who is perhaps excessively critical of his own perceived failings. This feature of the poem goes strangely unremarked in most commentary, and even when it's noted, it tends to be folded into one of the two standard interpretations. Writing in *The New Yorker*, for instance, the critic Dan Chiasson declares that the sigh represents "a later version of the self that this current version, though moving steadily in its direction, finds pitiable," and he declares the poem to be a "cunning nugget of nihilism." But one's self-image is only rarely accurate in the moment, let alone as a predictor of future behavior, and the poem itself provides no reason to conclude the speaker is "moving steadily" toward anything. We're no more bound to take his view of himself at face value than we are to believe Emma Bovary or Willy Loman.

It's important to remember that while "The Road Not Taken" isn't strictly "about" Edward Thomas, it was, at least, strongly associated with Thomas by Frost. And as the scholar Katherine Kearns rightly notes, Frost "by all accounts was genuinely fond of Thomas." Indeed, "Frost's protean ability to assume dramatic masks never elsewhere included such a friend as Thomas, whom he loved and admired, tellingly, more than 'anyone in England or anywhere else in the world.'" If you admire someone more than anyone "anywhere else in the world," you probably aren't going to link that person with a poem whose speaker comes off as either obnoxious or enfeebled. But you might well connect him with an exquisitely sensitive and self-aware speaker who thinks of himself—probably incorrectly—as fundamentally weak, and likely to behave in ways that will cause others to lose patience. "But you know already how I waver," Thomas wrote to Frost in early 1914, and "on what wavering things I depend." This is the figure who emerges between the two more common interpretations of "The Road Not Taken," and his doubting yet ardent sensibility is the secret warmth of the poem. This is what is, or can be, "absolutely saving."

———

POETRY HAS ALWAYS oscillated between guardedness and fervor. The effusions of Dylan Thomas give way to the ironies of Philip Larkin; the reticence of Elizabeth Bishop yields to the frenzy of Sylvia Plath; the closed becomes open; the hot grows cold. In this system of binaries, Frost has generally been regarded as not merely guarded, but practically encircled by battlements. In part this is a matter of temperament: His refusal to commit to positions can seem principled, in a roundabout way, but also evasive in a manner that Pound's *Cantos*, for all their difficulty, are not. There is a sense that, like Thomas Hardy, Frost sometimes saw himself as more allied with the impersonal forces often depicted in his poems than with the human characters those forces so frequently overwhelm. He isn't warm. He doesn't tell us what he's thinking. His poetry doesn't advertise its ambitions. "He presents," declares the introductory note on Frost in the second edition of *The Norton Anthology of Modern Poetry*, "an example of reserve or holding back in genre, diction, theme, and even philosophy, which is impressive but also, as seen after his death by a generation bent on extravagance, cautious."

"Cautious": not a word Frost would have liked. In his personal life, he was anything but, as is demonstrated by his nearly monomaniacal courtship of his wife, to say nothing of his decision to move to England at age thirty-eight on the basis of a coin toss. (He was much bolder in this regard than almost all of his modernist peers.) And the word seems equally inapplicable to his strongest writing, which is audacious in its willingness to engage multiple audiences (and be judged by them), as well as in its determination to display its technical wizardry in a way that was certain to be initially underestimated. It takes tremendous nerve to be willing to look as if you don't know what you're doing, when in fact you're a master of the activity in question. Even in 1915, for example, it was far from "cautious" for an ambitious poet to open his first book by deliberately rhyming "trees" with "breeze," a pairing so legendarily banal that it had been famously singled out for derision by Alexander Pope two hundred years earlier. True, Frost became tremendously successful by writing in the way he did, but success in a tricky venture doesn't make the venture itself any less risky.

Yet if the word "cautious" is wrong, it's interestingly

wrong. "The Road Not Taken" seems to be about the difficulty of decision making but is itself strangely reluctant to resolve. It keeps us in the woods, at the crossroads, unsure whether the speaker is actually even making a choice, and then ends not with the decision itself but with a claim about the future that seems unreliable. There is, in this sense, no road that "The Road Not Taken" fails to take. Is that desire to cover all possibilities "cautious"? Here it's useful to turn to another poem from Frost's early career, "Reluctance." That poem ends:

> Ah, when to the heart of man
>   Was it ever less than a treason
> To go with the drift of things,
>   To yield with a grace to reason,
> And bow and accept the end
>   Of a love or a season?

The conclusion of the poem is a protest against conclusions—an argument, you might say, for delay. But it's not an argument for caution, even though caution and delay are intertwined. After all, a stubborn sensibility also delays. A playful sensibility delays. An arrogant sensibility delays, because it won't be rushed. And while Frost can claim the greatest self-penned epitaph in the history of English-language poetry—I HAD A LOVER'S QUARREL WITH THE WORLD—it would have been no less accurate for his stone to have read STUBBORN, PLAYFUL, AND ARROGANT. Or even HE NEVER HURRIED.

"The Road Not Taken" isn't a poem that radiates this sort of confidence, obviously. But there is an overlap between its hesitations and evasions and the extent to which Frost, as a poet, simply doesn't like to leave the page. Here is Frost from an interview with *The Paris Review* in 1960, talking about the act of writing:

> The whole thing is performance and prowess and feats of association. Why don't critics talk about those things—what a feat it was to turn that that way, and what a feat it was to remember that, to be reminded of that by this? Why don't they talk about that? Scoring. You've got to *score*.

Poetry is frequently (endlessly, tediously) compared to music, but only rarely does one see it compared to ice hockey. Yet here is Frost—"You've got to *score*"—doing exactly that. This is of a piece with his famous quip that writing free verse is "like playing tennis without a net," a bon mot that is probably more interesting for its underlying metaphor (poets, those sedentary creatures, are like sportsmen) than for its actual claim. There is a sinewy, keyed-up athleticism to Frost's writing and, like all great athletes, he's reluctant to leave the field, which is, after all, the place he's most fully himself. Consider the end of his great love poem "To Earthward":

When stiff and sore and scarred
I take away my hand
From leaning on it hard
In grass and sand,

The hurt is not enough:
I long for weight and strength
To feel the earth as rough
To all my length.

Yes, these stanzas are about the hunger for sensation. But they're also about delay: Frost wants to feel the friction of love through the "length" of his body, but also to the "length" of his days, and through the "length" of the poem. Not just more touch, but more *time*.

And here is where Robert Frost and Edward Thomas (or Frost's idea of Thomas) are perhaps not so different. "The Road Not Taken" gives us several variations on the standard dilemmas associated with the romantic sensibility: How can one transcend one's self ("travel both") while still remaining oneself ("And be one traveler")? How can one ever arrive anywhere if one is constantly reaching for something purer ("the one less traveled by")? What is the difference between the stories we tell about ourselves and the actuality of our inner lives? In the moment of choosing—the moment of delay—all answers to these questions remain equally possible. But when a choice is made, other possibilities are foreclosed, which leads to what Frost describes as "crying over what might have been." So the romantic embraces delay ("long I stood / And looked down one as far as I could") because it postpones the inevitable loss. He hesitates like a candle flame wavers: hot but fragile, already wrapped in the smoke that will signal its extinction.

Both Frost and the speaker of "The Road Not Taken," then, are attracted to the idea of prolonging the moment of decision making (achieving a "momentary stay against confusion," as Frost would put it in a different context). The difference between them is one of attitude and degree. The speaker—and, by extension, Frost's conception of Thomas—is afraid of what he'll lose when the process of choosing ends, so he pauses over nearly any choice. Frost is afraid of losing the process itself, so he pauses over a decision that might result in genuine resolution—that might result, for instance, in a poem that is conclusive and immobile. He wants the ball to pass through the hoop, only to return to his hands, because for Frost the process—the continuation, the endless creation of endless roads—is everything. "No one," he writes, "can really hold that the ecstasy should be static and stand still in one place." You don't just have to score; you have to *keep scoring.*

———

BUT NO GAME CAN continue forever. Frost's fascination with delay allows him to understand the romantic sensibility, to sympathize with its fear of closure, even if its preoccupations aren't his own. And this understanding lets him create his own version of romantic yearning. This being Frost, of course, that yearning has very little in it of the "sigh" from "The Road Not Taken," or the overt regret that animates it. But it has a road, and the consequences of that road. Here is the beginning of "Directive," from 1946, which is usually considered to be Frost's last great poem:

> Back out of all this now too much for us,
> Back in a time made simple by the loss
> Of detail, burned, dissolved, and broken off
> Like graveyard marble sculpture in the weather,
> There is a house that is no more a house
> Upon a farm that is no more a farm
> And in a town that is no more a town.
> The road there, if you'll let a guide direct you

> *Who only has at heart your getting lost,*
> *May seem as if it should have been a quarry . . .*

The poem proceeds through a series of possible self-deceptions that recall the potential self-deceptions of "The Road Not Taken":

> *Make yourself up a cheering song of how*
> *Someone's road home from work this once was,*
> *Who may be just ahead of you on foot . . .*

These in turn give way to a scene of homecoming that hovers somewhere between parody and pathos:

> *Then make yourself at home. The only field*
> *Now left's no bigger than a harness gall.*
> *First there's the children's house of make-believe,*
> *Some shattered dishes underneath a pine,*
> *The playthings in the playhouse of the children.*
> *Weep for what little things could make them glad.*
> *Then for the house that is no more a house,*
> *But only a belilaced cellar hole,*
> *Now slowly closing like a dent in dough.*
> *This was no playhouse but a house in earnest.*

And the poem famously concludes with a cross between a baptism and the Grail quest:

I have kept hidden in the instep arch
Of an old cedar at the waterside
A broken drinking goblet like the Grail
Under a spell so the wrong ones can't find it,
So can't get saved, as Saint Mark says they mustn't.
(I stole the goblet from the children's playhouse.)
Here are your waters and your watering place.
Drink and be whole again beyond confusion.

As many critics have noted, "Directive" contains elements from dozens of Frost's earlier poems and critical pronounce-ments. But it's rarely connected with "The Road Not Taken"; indeed, the two are more likely to be contrasted than linked. Writing in *Slate*, for example, Robert Pinsky asserts that "works like 'The Road Not Taken' do not unsettle or revise any 19th-century notions of form or idea," whereas "Frost's greatest poems, such as 'Directive' and 'The Most of It,' do radically challenge and reimagine old conceptions of mem-ory, culture, and ways of beholding nature."

It's easy to see why some readers think this way. "Direc-tive" looks and feels both contemporary and significant. It shifts from one scene to another with little warning, it uses a motley palette of tones rather than one dominant, reliable voice, it's simultaneously rhetorical and punning ("no play-house but a house in earnest"), and it drops numerous hints that it should be categorized as a Major Work. When

David Lehman, the editor of the *Best American Poetry* series, asked his guest editors—all eminent contemporary poets— to name the greatest American poems of the century, "Directive" was one of three Frost poems to receive multiple votes. "The Road Not Taken" didn't make the list, although it was named America's favorite poem by the thousands of readers who participated in Pinsky's Favorite Poem Project. This is to be expected. "Directive" has become the poem that dedicated readers—the same readers who consider "The Road Not Taken" a minor, dark joke—most admire. "This is the poem," Frost told an early biographer, "that converted the other group [the followers of T. S. Eliot]. There I rest my case." It makes sense, then, that "Directive" continues to impress Eliot's heirs. Reading it, you feel that if John Ashbery were to write a Robert Frost poem, this is what it would sound like.

And yet there is good reason to connect the much celebrated "Directive" with the frequently derided "The Road Not Taken." "Directive" is the poem in which Frost makes his way back to the crossroads—but as an approximation of himself, not as a version of Edward Thomas. It's a poem about the aftermath of choice: It is Frost's version of the "sigh." In exploring the domestic tragedies that are often considered to be sources for the poem's central images, Mark Richardson argues, "it is not going too far to say that in 'Directive' Frost returns to the scene of the crime, so to speak, and that he has come here to ask, in light of the patently 'liturgical' qualities of the poem, to be shriven." Richardson then quotes Reuben Brower, one of Frost's old students, who claims "Directive" is a return "to the beginning of his life and his poetry, but it is a return after having taken one road rather than another"—an echo from "The Road Not Taken" that is revealing even if unintentional.

Both poems rely on the image of an unreliable road that is imperfectly understood by its traveler. "Directive" contains a guide, true, but that guide "only has at heart your getting lost" and may be understood not just as the poet leading the reader, but as a past version of the same traveler guiding the current version. (Read this way, in the line "Back out of all this now too much for us," the "us" becomes a variant of the royal "we.") But the most important overlap between the two poems occurs in the hypnotic concluding lines of "Directive." The guide tells us that he has hidden "a broken drinking goblet like the Grail" so that "the wrong ones can't find it, / So can't get saved, as Saint Mark says they mustn't." Frost is referring to Mark 4:11–12, in which Jesus explains why he speaks in parables:

> And he said unto them, Unto you it is given to know the mystery of the kingdom of God: but unto them that are without, all these things are done in parables: That seeing they may see, and not perceive; and hearing they may hear, and not understand; lest at any

time they should be converted, and their sins should
be forgiven them.

For Frost, these lines were equally applicable to poetry, which
some people would simply never understand, and which even
good readers needed to approach in the right way. A poem,
then, becomes a way to separate an audience into factions.

The same idea emerges in two ways in "The Road Not
Taken." First, as discussed earlier, the speaker focuses solely
on the amount of travel each road received (rather than on
the roads' relative steepness or narrowness and so forth),
which means his selection between them involves separating
himself from other people. The road isn't just a choice; it's
a choice premised on exclusion. Second, that choice is mir-
rored in the larger subterfuges of the poem itself, in the way
it encourages interpretations, only to undercut them, sepa-
rating readers into those who thought they understood, oth-
ers who thought those readers *didn't* understand, and so on
in a nearly endless cycle. As Frost wrote to Louis Unter-
meyer, "I'll bet not half a dozen people can tell who was hit
and where he was hit by my Road Not Taken."

———

BUT AS WE'VE SEEN, "who was hit and where he was hit" is
nearly impossible to determine. This is because "The Road

Not Taken" isn't a joke but a poem. A joke (or trick) has a right answer, but a poem only has answers that are better or worse—a point that is relevant to the most important connection between "Directive" and "The Road Not Taken." Recall the beginning of the latter poem:

> *Two roads diverged in a yellow wood,*
> *And sorry I could not travel both*
> *And be one traveler . . .*

And recall the conclusion of "Directive":

> *Here are your waters and your watering place.*
> *Drink and be whole again beyond confusion.*

The poem's final line is an overt reference to Frost's well-known description of a successful poem's ending as "a momentary stay against confusion." But why the word "whole"? And why "again"? The suggestion appears to be that the "you" of the poem, though previously one entity, has somehow become divided.

Divided, we might say, by the road taken. Divided when the process of choosing gives way to the fact of choice.

The Choice

The mind is a baby giant who, more provident in the cradle than he knows, has hurled his paths in life all round ahead of him like playthings. . . . They are vocabulary, grammar, prosody, and diary, and it will be too bad if he can't find stepping stones of them for his feet wherever he wants to go. The way will be zigzag, but it will be a straight crookedness like the walking stick he cuts himself in the bushes for an emblem. He will be judged as he does or doesn't let this zig or that zag project him off out of his general direction.

FROST, "THE CONSTANT SYMBOL,"
The Atlantic Monthly, *October 1946*

What does it mean to make a decision? This is perhaps the only question to be debated with equal intensity by neuroscientists, business executives, philosophers, economists, game show contestants, and married couples, and it's unlikely to be resolved by, of all things, a poem. Nor would this be surprising even if the question were a much simpler or more poetic one—something about melancholia or spring, for example. As a general matter, poems aren't good at resolving dilemmas.

They are, however, very good at illustrating concepts—or maybe *embodying* them would be a better way to put it. Typically the concepts in question involve the standard themes of English literature (love, mortality, justice), and the resulting form is one we respond to as if guided by an instinct we didn't realize we possessed. As Samuel Johnson puts it in describing Thomas Gray's "Elegy Written in a Country Churchyard," the poem "abounds with images which find a mirror in every breast; and with sentiments to which every bosom returns an echo." As Johnson sees it, we don't just read Gray's great meditation on death—"Full many a flow'r is born to blush unseen, / And waste its sweetness on the desert air"—we recognize it.

And at first, this is exactly what appears to occur when we read "The Road Not Taken." The poem seems like a piece of sea glass washed up from the shadowy waters of the subconscious, every inch of which has been slowly etched with an archetypal representation of decision making: a dark forest, a lonely road, a solitary traveler, a crossroads, an "either" and an "or." "Two roads diverged in a yellow wood, / And sorry I could not travel both"—within two lines, it feels as if we've arrived at the center of the dilemma intrinsic to all dilemmas: the necessity of choice itself. If we were to dream about what it means to choose, that dream would look something like "The Road Not Taken."

Yet it's worth wondering why this is so. After all, while it's certainly right to say that "The Road Not Taken" gives us a portrait of choice, the depiction it offers is of an extraordinarily narrow sort. This can be an easy thing to miss. As the poet Paul Muldoon once remarked, the poem "just flies off the page," and the easy unfolding of its lines can make us forget the many aspects of choosing that the poem manages to rule out. There are quite a lot of them, as it happens, and it's helpful to recall those missing aspects when we're considering how choice is actually being presented. In "The Road Not Taken," we do *not* find:

Other people. Though Frost doesn't make the speaker's solitude explicit, it seems reasonable to infer from the text ("long *I* stood"). So the decision between the two roads takes place without consultation with, or influence from, anyone else. Nor does the speaker's choice affect anyone else—this is not a decision that involves a family, or compels a battalion.

Culture. The roads are in a wood, not a city or a neighborhood or a strip mall or an industrial park. There are no signs at the crossroads. There are no pamphlets. There is no cairn or sculpture or pink plastic flamingo.

The speaker doesn't overhear a radio broadcast or get a glimpse of a projected image. While the speaker is surely influenced by previous cultural experiences, culture plays no immediate role in his decision.

Pressure. The speaker is presented as being more or less at his leisure, rather than, say, being pursued by a bear or needing to choose the correct road in order to reach the only medical equipment that can save the life of his friend, who fell into a ravine half a mile back.

Distraction. The speaker is able to focus completely on his choice. He's not simultaneously trying to re-member a birthday, count the change in his pocket, mentally compose a letter, rearrange his backpack, or look for trail markers.

Moral consequences. The speaker isn't choosing be-tween, on the one hand, a road that will enable him to save the life of a person he knows and, on the other, a road that will enable him to save the lives of fifteen strangers.

Multiple options. There are only two roads, not three or four. And the two roads don't offer obvious addi-tional options, as might be the case if, for instance, the speaker could see that one of the roads branched into two more roads only a hundred feet down the trail.

Options that lack differentiating qualities. True, the two roads are worn "really about the same" and "equally lay / In leaves," but this doesn't mean the roads are indiscernible. By contrast, consider choosing among cans of Campbell's tomato soup at the grocery store, or among individual pieces of white paper in a five-hundred-sheet pack.

Trivial options. For instance, the speaker isn't debating whether to begin walking by stepping with his right foot or with his left, or what tune to whistle as he strolls on. Yet consider how many of our daily decisions are of precisely this minor sort.

A choice not to choose. At no point does Frost suggest that the speaker might simply turn around or sit down or blaze a trail separate from the roads (an action that would arguably be more in keeping with the poem's traditional interpretation as a monument to individualism).

So if all these potential dimensions of choice (a list that could easily be longer) are missing from the poem, what are we left with? A kind of idealized or "pure" choice. A choice from which most of the factors that can complicate or undermine individual decision making have been deliberately withheld. A choice, then, that seems to occur in perfect laboratory conditions for testing a very old idea: that a free agent acting freely can make a decision that matters.

——————

WHICH IS A NOTION that has long been central to Western civilization, particularly in its late-blossoming manifestation in the United States. Indeed, the theme of choosing runs through American history and culture at least as deeply as its close cousins freedom and individualism. The Declaration of Independence declares the "pursuit of happiness" to be a natural right, which presupposes that there are choices that would make such a pursuit possible. (To pursue, after all, it is necessary to choose.) John Adams defines individual liberty as "a self-determining power in an intellectual agent. It implies thought and choice"—a way of thinking that is essential to the democratic process, however imperfectly it may be realized in practice. The more one thinks about Adams's "self-determining power," the more it seems inseparable from most of the values and ideas that underpin (or are usually said to underpin) American society. Alexis de Tocqueville, for example, claims that the people of the United States are distinguished by their belief in human perfectability, a concept that assumes the humans in question can make choices that will lead to improvement. As he puts it, "Thus, forever seeking, forever falling to rise again, often disappointed, but not discouraged, [the American] tends unceasingly towards that unmeasured greatness so indistinctly visible at the end of the long track which humanity has yet to tread."

To believe in progress, as Tocqueville conceives of it, is to believe in choice: American optimism is rooted in American confidence in individual decision making. It's a sentiment that is echoed at the end of *The Great Gatsby*, a great American novel that is also one of the great novels of choosing:

> [Gatsby] had come a long way to this blue lawn and his dream must have seemed so close that he could hardly fail to grasp it. He did not know that it was already behind him, somewhere back in that vast obscurity beyond the city, where the dark fields of the republic rolled on under the night.
>
> Gatsby believed in the green light, the orgiastic future that year by year recedes before us. It eluded us then, but that's no matter—tomorrow we will run faster, stretch out our arms farther. . . .

Someday, then, we will choose differently. And it will, we believe, make all the difference. So it's no surprise to see thirteen million Americans eager to watch LeBron James choose a basketball team in a television special called "The Decision," or similar numbers of people willing to watch

The Bachelor, in which a man systematically (some would say relentlessly) chooses a marriage partner from a pool of twenty-five contestants. It's no surprise that a series of American young adult books built around multiple story lines would be called *Choose Your Own Adventure* (rather than say, *Endless Stories*) or that more than 250 million of them would be in print by the late 1990s. It's no surprise that one of the hymns most closely associated with the crusades of the Reverend Billy Graham ("America's pastor") would be "I Have Decided to Follow Jesus." We're more interested in stories about consequences that come from choosing than in stories about chance, or mere survival. *Jaws* wouldn't be *Jaws* without the mayor's foolish decision to keep the beaches of Amity Island open, or Quint's maniacal choice to destroy his boat's engine in the film's closing moments. (The movie is at least as much about bad decision making as it is about a giant fish.) In *The Godfather,* Michael's fall into crime is conspicuously the result of a choice: He is given another option, another life, and he turns away. Luke Skywalker, dangling from a broken railing, decides to refuse Darth Vader's proffered hand. "It could have been otherwise," each film seems to say, "but for this choice." And if choice is what we want from screenplays, it's also what we want in the dramas of our own lives: We want to choose, and to be seen choosing. We want it our way, to paraphrase Burger King, and we want others to know that we actually got it our way, to paraphrase Paul Anka (and Frank Sinatra).

Not all choices are the same, obviously. But they are joined, as Frost intuited, by our belief that they follow a similar pattern: We observe, we consciously evaluate, we choose between or among competing options. The choice, as they say, is ours. And implicated in that belief is a distinctive way of looking at the world and ourselves. Researchers who study cross-cultural attitudes routinely find that the United States is one of the most individualistic countries in the world— if not *the* most—and that its individualism is linked with an unusually high acceptance of status stratification. (In cross-cultural research, the combination of these traits is referred to as a VI culture—Vertical, Individualistic—and the United States is sometimes described as the "quintessential" example.) In 2002, Pew Research Center polled dozens of countries on the following question as part of its Global Attitudes Project: "Some say that most people who don't succeed in life fail because of society's failures. Others say that most people who don't succeed do so because of their own individual failures. Which comes closer to your point of view?" Eighty-two percent of the respondents in the United States answered "individual failure," putting the U.S. ahead of every country but the Czech Republic, which had the same score.

———

As one might expect, then, choice has become a subject of relentless, nearly overwhelming interest to Western audiences, and especially to American audiences. One of the most straightforward ways to get a sense of the intensity and range of that interest is simply to type "how to make decisions" into the Amazon.com search bar. This will give you, among many other titles, such helpful books as:

Decisive: How to Make Better Choices in Life and Work

Winning Decisions: Getting It Right the First Time

Smart Choices: A Practical Guide to Making Better Decisions

Mental Training: The Art of Life and Death Decision Making

Eyes Wide Open: How to Make Smart Decisions in a Confusing World

Risk Savvy: How to Make Good Decisions

Make Up Your Mind: A Decision Making Guide to Thinking Clearly and Choosing Wisely

Decisions: How to Make the Best Choice Every Time

Power of Decision: How to Make Better Decisions Every Day

How to Make "Choice" Decisions: Discover How to Make the Right Decisions All the Time

And so on. If the speaker of "The Road Not Taken" had the benefit of this reading list, the poem might have ended after two lines: "Two roads diverged in a yellow wood / And I took the correct one, after carefully weighing all factors to maximize expected utility."

These how-to books reflect a much deeper engagement with choice in the university system—an engagement that spans a startling number of academic departments. The Society for Judgment and Decision Making, for example, is an interdisciplinary group that has existed since 1980 and publishes a journal called, unsurprisingly, *Judgment and Decision Making*. A typical issue is filled with a mix of business school professors, psychologists, statisticians, economists, and neuroscientists writing on subjects that range from "Would You Rather Be Injured by Lightning or a Downed Power Line?: Preference for Natural Hazards" to "Why Are Gainers More Risk Seeking?" The wide range of authors and subjects is perhaps unavoidable. As William Goldstein and Robin Hogarth put it in their survey *Research in Judgment and Decision Making* nearly twenty years ago:

JDM [Judgment and Decision Making] research is not "paradigmatic." There is no single, universally endorsed, overarching theoretical framework that researchers use to organize and guide their efforts. Rather, there are a number of schools of thought that identify different issues as interesting and deem different methods as appropriate. In addition, the situation is complicated by the fact that these schools overlap and interact.

"Overlap and interact" may be putting it mildly: The idea of choice is so vast, and its contours so uncertain, that mapping any portion of it requires tools ranging from the practical (the computer, for most academics) to the vanishingly abstract. So when, for example, Shane Frederick, a professor of marketing at Yale, publishes an article entitled "Time Preference and Personal Identity" in *Time and Decision,* it seems perfectly natural for that article to include a lengthy discussion of the philosopher Derek Parfit's conception of the self. By the same token, when Richard Holton, a philosopher at Oxford, writes an article entitled "The Act of Choice," that essay depends on citations of experiments by a squadron of psychologists and neuroscientists. Choice is large, it seems, and it contains multitudes.

So large, in fact, that our fascination with it can support

a very large body of general interest books that focus not sim-
ply on the best way to decide but on the mechanisms that
make decision possible in the first place. These are books that
try to answer the question "How?" rather than "How to?" and
they include titles like Jonah Lehrer's *How We Decide*, Read
Montague's *Your Brain Is (Almost) Perfect: How We Make
Decisions*, Dan Ariely's *Predictably Irrational: The Hidden
Forces That Shape Our Decisions*, and Gary Klein's *Sources
of Power: How People Make Decisions*. This phenomenon
is more unusual than it might at first seem. Typically, the
foundational aspects of a given subject are of more interest
to academics than to general readers: Yes, we'd like to know
about music theory or about how the brain works when lis-
tening to music, but books on those subjects are dwarfed by
those devoted to the history of rap, Bob Dylan's acoustic
period, how to play the guitar in twelve easy steps, or what
have you. Where choice is concerned, however, the most basic
questions—definitional questions, even—become strangely
compelling. It's as if, when we talk about choice, we're inter-
ested not just in the roads we take or fail to take, but what we
mean by "taking a road." At the root of this is an anxiety that
appears all the stronger for being largely implicit.

Consider, for instance, *The Art of Choosing*, by Sheena
Iyengar. Iyengar is a professor at Columbia Business School
who is well known for, among other things, having conducted

what's often referred to as "the jam study." In that experiment, Iyengar and her coauthors demonstrated that, contrary to prevailing wisdom in the business community, consumers would purchase more jam if offered fewer flavors—that a plethora of choices led to discontentedness, not greater pleasure. As one might expect, her book is an intriguing examination of common assumptions about choice that turn out to be incorrect, inadequate, or beside the point. Does it seem as if the American emphasis on individual choice isn't really "American" so much as simply "human"? No, says Iyengar, our notion of choice is deeply modified by culture, in particular whether our culture is more strongly oriented toward individualism or collectivism. Isn't it true that our choices help us to form consistent, pleasingly unique selves? Well, no, Iyengar reveals: We don't really want to be unique, and our perception of internal consistency is often an illusion, albeit a helpful one. But at least when we make choices, surely we do so by applying memory, or common sense? Alas, in actuality we're more likely resorting to a heuristic that we've absorbed unconsciously and that may well lead us into an unhelpful bias.

This potentially unnerving news is delivered through such lively, fascinating anecdotes and with a tone of such cheerful reasonableness that it's easy to fail to notice that the idea of choice—as most people understand it, anyway—has been significantly undermined. By the book's end, Iyengar has thoroughly demonstrated that, as she puts it, we "cannot take full measure" of choice, so it seems a little confusing when she nonetheless concludes, "Science can help us become better choosers." One wonders whether "help" is really the right word for what science is offering. That feeling grows stronger when Iyengar asks us, in keeping with the goal of becoming "better choosers," to think about the end of Camus's famous essay "The Myth of Sisyphus." Sisyphus, of course, was condemned to push a rock up a slope for eternity, and Camus argues that, despite this seemingly hopeless scenario, "one must imagine him happy." Iyengar suggests that we, too, should "reach for the heights and for happiness through choice." When you find yourself talking about Camus and Sisyphus in this context, you've strayed rather far from the idea of choice most people would like to believe in. It's the kind of comparison that makes a reader begin to wonder how much deciding there really is in decision making.

That question is confronted somewhat more directly in other books about choosing, most recently *The Myth of Choice*, by Kent Greenfield, a law professor at Boston College. Lawyers are interested in choice for the obvious reason that blame is typically apportioned according to perceived responsibility, and responsibility is often assumed to flow from individual decisions. If two roads diverge in a wood, and we take the one that cuts through someone's private property, where we proceed to unintentionally knock over someone's valuable outdoor sculpture, well, we had better get our checkbook out. Greenfield is aware of the many constraints on choice that Iyengar covers, and he discusses them in helpful detail, with the goal of recommending a legal regime that acknowledges the difficulty of attributing responsibility when causation is hazy. Yet he goes a step further: "But despite our feelings, brain science is revealing that our decision making processes are much more bewildering than we ever imagined, and that our own perceptions of free will should not necessarily be trusted." Which is to say, we might not have free will at all. The psychologist Dan Ariely is equally frank in the last few pages of *Predictably Irrational*:

> If I were to distill one main lesson from the research described in this book, it is that we are pawns in a game whose forces we largely fail to comprehend. We usually think of ourselves as sitting in the driver's seat, with ultimate control over the decisions we make and the direction our life takes; but, alas, this perception has more to do with our desires—with how we want to view ourselves—than with reality.

Of course, not many people enjoy hearing that they lead the life of an unwitting pawn, which perhaps explains why

Ariely quickly qualifies this judgment: "Although irrationality is commonplace, it does not necessarily mean that we are helpless." A curious pattern emerges in many of these books: The author puts forward a convincing argument that choice as we usually understand it is largely an illusion, then he quickly shifts tracks, suggesting that somehow, by becoming more aware of its illusory nature, we can make it more concrete. The "how" becomes a "how to," probably because most authors intuit that people want to know about the machinery of choice only if it turns out that they can put at least a finger on the controls. Thus Greenfield, having tiptoed up to the proposition that genuine choice is impossible, retreats in the end to the idea that, actually, choice just "takes effort, and we can be good or bad at it." It is, in other words, a *real* thing, however bewildering it may be, and we can improve ourselves by thinking harder about it. Only minutes from our appointment with Sisyphus, we're abruptly rescued by Dr. Phil.

———

ONE OF THE MORE CURIOUS aspects of "The Road Not Taken," as I suggested in the last chapter, is its ambiguous title. Which road *was* taken, and by whom? And which road, the taken or the un-, should we be concerned with? The title suggests an uncertainty regarding not just the specific choice made by the speaker, but the nature of choice itself, and a deep appreciation for its potential instability as a concept.

It's an uncertainty that Frost fully understood and, to the extent it's meaningful to say so, chose. Frost's prose remarks on the concept of choice, like much of his other prose, are probably best described as "uncommitted"—and, given Frost's fondness for misdirection, contradiction, and play, that's hardly surprising. On one hand, there is ample evidence that Frost considered himself the prime mover in his own life to a degree that many people would find nearly unbearable. (He unhesitatingly blamed himself for the death of his and Elinor's first child, for example.) On the other hand, Frost was remarkably open to the idea that many of the things he did were not consciously contrived and, indeed, occurred because of processes from which his conscious deliberations were entirely excluded. As he puts it in a note collected by David H. Lowenherz and reprinted by Donald Sheehy in *The Cambridge Companion to Robert Frost*:

I never know what is going to happen next because I don't dare to let myself formulate a foolish hope. Much less do I know what is happening now: I am too flooded with feeling to know. I suppose I live chiefly in the past, in realizing what happened and taking

credit for it just as if I had predetermined it and con-
sciously carried it out. But Lord Lord—I am never the
creature of high resolve you want to have me. I have
simply go[ne] the way of the dim beliefs I speak of
dimly because I don't want them brought out into the
light and examined too exactly. They won't bear it I
may as well admit to forestall ridicule.

"In realizing what happened and taking credit for it": This
comment, made in 1939, is essentially a restatement of the
first lines of the final stanza of "The Road Not Taken" ("I
shall be telling this with a sigh / Somewhere ages and ages
hence"). Frost carefully works a sliver of doubt into the space
between what has occurred in our lives and what we will tell
ourselves we chose.

That doubt—or, to put it more optimistically, that open
space for multiple possibilities—was central to much of
Frost's best poetry. In *Robert Frost: The Work of Knowing*,
Richard Poirier provides an especially helpful analysis of
this aspect of Frost's work and how it emerges from the poet's
peculiar relationship with choice. Poirier takes his cue from
the final stanza of "The Trial by Existence":

> *'Tis of the essence of life here,*
> *Though we choose greatly, still to lack*

> *The lasting memory at all clear,*
> *That life has for us on the wrack*
> *Nothing but what we somehow chose;*
> *Thus are we wholly stripped of pride*
> *In the pain that has but one close,*
> *Bearing it crushed and mystified.*

Frost, Poirier argues, is distinguishing between what we "choose greatly" and what we "somehow chose," the latter of which encompasses the former. Poirier elaborates:

> The pride we may take in conscious choices is stripped away not by any obvious predominance of the unconscious ones but rather by our being ignorant of how much more inclusive they [the unconscious choices] are. That is, the individual is denied the *privilege* of knowing that in fact no one else has made his life as it is. Frost was always seeking for the restitution of that lost and diminished sense of responsibility even while he was at the same time exalted by the mystery of not being able fully to grasp it.

We can't accurately tell the stories of our own choices, Frost might say, but they are nonetheless ours, and there is something pleasing—or at any rate fascinating—in the way we fall short of understanding them consciously, and in the hope that we might somehow *not* fall short. In our reaching and failing we create a life, a story, an art.

———

WE ALSO, one might say, create a deception. But this seems a little harsh. Better, maybe, to say that we create a narrative that works for us, and that we can live with. It's interesting, in light of this, to think about the phenomenon scientists call confabulation. Confabulation isn't lying, as you might suppose, but rather the invention of explanations or stories on the basis of information that is incomplete, incorrect, or manipulated (as in an experiment, for instance). A person who is confabulating may be saying something thoroughly ridiculous, but he doesn't actually know that it's absurd. He's simply expressing the best available conception of the world as it seems to him, and he believes in that conception unswervingly. "Confabulation," writes the philosopher William Hirstein, ". . . is a sort of pathological certainty about ill-grounded thoughts and utterances."

Of course, certainty about "the world as it seems to him or her" will seem especially strange if the person in question has suffered some kind of neurological damage. This is why many of the best-known studies of confabulation involve a parade of unfortunate medical conditions like Korsakoff's syndrome (sufferers have lost short-term autobiographical memory), anosognosia (in which a paralyzed person appears unaware of his condition), asomatognosia (the sufferer denies ownership of his own body parts), and the legendarily bizarre Capgras syndrome (in which a person believes friends and loved ones have been replaced with physically identical impostors). In each of these cases the patient will, with perfect confidence, provide explanations for various occurrences that are, on their face, impossible—for instance, a person suffering from Korsakoff's might, if asked what he did yesterday, answer by reciting events that occurred to him twenty years ago.

But where Frost and "The Road Not Taken" are concerned, the most salient examples of confabulation come from so-called split-brain research. Normally, the hemispheres of the brain are connected by a band of neural fibers called the corpus callosum, the function of which is to facilitate communication between the two halves. The corpus callosum of a person with a split brain has been severed, such that the hemispheres can no longer exchange information as they normally would—in effect, the person now has two brains. In a famous series of experiments from the late seventies, the neuropsychologists Michael Gazzaniga and Joseph LeDoux helped show that this condition can lead to confabulation so spectacular that it seems to say something essential and unsettling about the way we handle choices.

In order to understand Gazzaniga and LeDoux's results,

it's necessary to bear in mind two facts about human biology. The first is that the brain's control of the human body is contralateral, which is to say, the left hemisphere of the brain controls the right side of the body, and the right hemisphere controls the left. The second is that speech is centered in the brain's left hemisphere, so information that reaches only the right hemisphere of a split-brain subject literally cannot be talked about (though the right hemisphere can, for example, use the hand it controls to draw a picture of an image it can't verbalize).

Gazzaniga and LeDoux's experiments relied on this bifurcation. They asked split-brain subjects to look straight ahead while images were flashed quickly in their right and left fields of vision. Because the images appeared in non-overlapping areas of the visual field and vanished before the subject's eyes could move, the scientists were able to send images directly to one hemisphere while preventing the other from receiving the image at all (because, of course, the hemispheres couldn't communicate with each other). Here is what happened with a subject called P.S., as Gazzaniga describes it in *Who's in Charge? Free Will and the Science of the Brain*:

> We showed . . . two pictures: A chicken claw was shown to his right visual field, so the left hemisphere only saw the claw picture, and a snow scene was shown

to the left visual field, so the right hemisphere only saw that. He was then asked to choose a picture from an array of pictures placed in full view in front of him, which both hemispheres could see. The left hand pointed to a shovel (which was the most appropriate answer for the snow scene) and the right hand pointed to a chicken (the most appropriate answer for the chicken claw).

Then we asked why he chose those items. His left-hemisphere speech center replied, "Oh, that's simple. The chicken claw goes with the chicken," easily explaining what it knew. . . . Then, looking down at his left hand pointing to the shovel, without missing a beat, he said, "And you need a shovel to clean out the chicken shed."

As Gazzaniga goes on to observe, "What was interesting was that the left hemisphere did not say, 'I don't know,' which truly was the correct answer. It made up a post hoc answer that fit the situation." Or as Frost might put it, the left hemisphere realized what had happened—which road had been chosen—and took credit for it. It made up an impressively creative story to fit the reality that it perceived, one it might be telling "ages and ages hence."

And this, we are beginning to realize, is a much more common occurrence than anyone had thought. More recently, psychologists have done substantial research on what is known as choice blindness, which, as its name suggests, is a kind of inability to "see" a decision. The lack of perception in question doesn't have to do with aspects of a choice in progress, however, but with the nature of a choice already made: We literally cannot perceive what it is that we have chosen. In the best-known experiment on this phenomenon, the Swedish researchers Petter Johansson and Lars Hall gave a group of volunteers a series of paired photographs of female faces and asked the subjects to pick which woman in each pair they found more attractive. The researchers would then show the subjects the same card they had just chosen, and in some cases the subject would be asked to supply reasons for his or her decision. Each person looked at fifteen pairs of faces and made fifteen choices—but for three of the pairs, the researchers used a card trick to switch the faces after the volunteer's selection. So in effect, the chooser was given the opposite of the choice he or she had actually made.

The researchers found, first, that the rate of detection for the swaps was shockingly low—of 354 manipulated trials, only 46—or 13 percent—were immediately discovered by the volunteers. Second, the subjects were no better at remembering choices between dissimilar faces than they were at recalling choices between faces that resembled one another. Finally, when asked to explain their falsified choices, the subjects used a range of confabulations that not only echoed the reasoning they used to support their "real" choices but in some cases involved rejecting features of their actual selections. For example, after having picked a photo of a woman with no visible jewelry, one male subject was then given a picture of a woman wearing very large hoop earrings. He promptly explained that he had chosen as he had because "I like earrings!" Perhaps even stranger were the confabulations that involved attributing a feature to the manipulated image that was actually present only in the originally chosen picture. One female subject declared that she had selected a picture of an unsmiling woman "because she was smiling"— as the subject's first choice had in fact been. Subsequent experiments have demonstrated that people are generally unable to detect reversals of their own prior stated choices with respect to the taste of jam, the smell of tea, abstract art patterns, monetary gambles, and even political/moral positions. They are perfectly willing to offer elaborate stories to support choices they didn't make, and to criticize choices they made. Indeed, they are happy to offer ex post facto explanations for just about anything. Which returns us to one of the questions at the heart of "The Road Not Taken": If we don't understand why we made a decision—if we don't know why we "took the other, as just as fair"—then how can our choices be meaningful?

THE DEBATE OVER free will and determinism is ancient. The Greeks first framed it; as Leucippus remarked in the fifth century B.C., "Nothing comes to be at random, but everything for a reason and by necessity," which leaves little room for human agency. And Epictetus asked, "How do events happen? They happen as the Disposer of events has ordained them," thereby giving us the essence of several hundred years of arguments over divine foreknowledge. But for modern readers, the most relevant early description of determinism comes from the Stoic philosopher Chrysippus:

> Everything that happens is followed by something else which depends on it by causal necessity. Likewise, everything that happens is preceded by something with which it is causally connected. For nothing exists or has come into being in the cosmos without a cause.

This is what philosophers call causal determinism—the idea that, as the *Stanford Encyclopedia of Philosophy* puts it, "every event is necessitated by antecedent events and conditions together with the laws of nature." This view is what prompts Gazzaniga to say that "the concept of free will is without meaning." It is what leads the biologist Jerry Coyne to assert, "No, we couldn't have had that V8, and Robert Frost couldn't have taken the other road." If phenomena like choice blindness suggest that we may not understand our own choices (which is disconcerting enough), determinism suggests that whatever choice we make is the only choice we could have made—and therefore, arguably, it is no choice at all. It's the disquieting possibility from which so many books on choosing shy away in their closing moments.

While science has yet to prove that the universe is mechanistic, the evidence thus far has rarely been helpful for free will, at least as it is popularly understood. In particular, a series of experiments reaching back to the early eighties have shown (with caveats) that unconscious neural activity in the brain seems to precede our conscious awareness of having made a decision, in some cases by as much as seven seconds. Benjamin Libet was one of the first scientists to study this effect; in a seminal study from 1983, he found that a subject's conscious intent to make small finger movements came only after certain neural processes had already indicated the movement would occur. That finding has generally been supported by subsequent researchers, including the neuroscientist Itzhak Fried, who was able to predict with roughly 80 percent accuracy which of two buttons a subject would press before the subject reported he or she had consciously decided to do so. More recently, researchers have found that the unconscious activity isn't limited to small motor movements, but also occurs when volunteers are asked to choose whether to add or subtract a given series of numbers. This allowed the scientists to predict the subjects' choices "considerably better than you would expect by chance," as one of them put it. The study, by John-Dylan Haynes and Chun Siong Soon, is called "Predicting Free Choices for Abstract Intentions," and the unintentionally disturbing title is of a piece with the sense one gets, in reading neuroscientific literature, that the idea of choice may soon be preserved only by defining it out of recognition.

Of course, deciding how concepts should be defined— and whether it makes sense to continue using them—has traditionally been the job of philosophers, not scientists. Against the backdrop of these scientific advances, contemporary philosophers have positioned themselves on the border of determinism and free will in an increasingly baroque and clashing array, like a mosaic composed of mutually repelling magnets. Each of these magnets has a very specific designation. There are hard incompatibilists, soft incompatibilists, compatibilists, semicompatibilists, libertarians (not the political sort), hard determinists, impossibilists, illusionists, and on and on. (It's difficult here not to pull for the so-called daring soft libertarians, if only because their name makes them sound like slightly naughty throw rugs.) For present purposes, it isn't necessary for us to understand every aspect of these approaches, many of which have the intricacy of Swiss watches. It's enough to say that nearly all of them can be accommodated by "The Road Not Taken." Consider the way in which the poem encompasses the following positions, two of which are diametrically opposed:

A Hard Determinist believes that the world is causally determined, and that free will is an illusion. "The Road Not Taken" can easily be read as giving us a speaker who makes the choice he was always going to make, and who will later engage in after-the-fact justification.

Libertarians believe that determinism is incompatible with genuinely free will, that we *do* have such free will, and that determinism is therefore false. This position is in line with the popular interpretation of the poem as a choice made by an empowered, self-determining speaker who will later know that his decisions made "all the difference" in his own life.

Compatibilists (the majority of contemporary philosophers) think that some variant of determinism is likely true, but that we nonetheless have free will—though a very different sort of free will than people usually assume. A compatibilist might say that the speaker took the road he selected because of his own beliefs and desires, and so his choice was in that sense free.

And so on. When one considers the enormous complexity of the issues surrounding decision making and the sheer amount of disagreement about how and why we choose, it is staggering to see how effortlessly Frost's seemingly simple poem holds every perspective in equal regard. It's as if, from the depths of 1915, the poet anticipated not just the arguments that people would make a hundred years later, but the vast shadow that dispute would cast over the culture.

Because we are living, as it's become a cliché to say, in an age of choice. And yet it can also seem like an age of limitation. Consider a service like Amazon.com. Surely there have never been more digital cameras, running socks, spatulas, and facial moisturizers placed simultaneously before more people in more places in the history of humanity. But because our decisions are relentlessly tracked and fed into algorithms, the choices that will be highlighted for us in the future become increasingly narrow. (Amazon has actually patented a service called "anticipatory shipping," which would predict customers' orders and possibly even go so far as to send them out for delivery before an order is even placed—the overlap here with the predictive ambitions of neuroscience is obvious, if slightly alarming.) Our choices can be liberating ("all the difference"), but they can also be confining, as if we were not brave, free souls standing at our ease before a crossroads, but rather rats running through a tapering maze. It is hard not to feel as if something more than simply the act of choice or the idea of free will is at stake in these debates. Because choices, we think, don't simply happen in the way that snoring or sweating or pupil dilation occurs. No, there is always something behind a choice; something that seems dear to us, and worth protecting. There is the chooser.

The Chooser

They would not find me changed from him they knew—
Only more sure of all I thought was true.

FROST, "INTO MY OWN"

On April 18, 2006, during the height of the American occupation of Iraq, President George W. Bush was asked repeatedly by reporters about the status of Donald Rumsfeld, the secretary of defense. Many of Rumsfeld's predictions about the course of the invasion had proved to be, let us say, optimistic, and a number of former generals had publicly questioned his leadership. How do you respond, the reporters asked Bush, to critics who think that Rumsfeld should be removed? The president shook his head and grunted out a laugh. He said, "I hear the voices, and I read the front page, and I know the speculation." He tapped the podium with the side of his hand. "But I'm the decider, and I decide what is best."

It was a moment that would come to haunt his presidency. *The Daily Show* promptly ran an animated parody portraying Bush as a superhero known as "The Decider," and this was soon followed by another episode called "The Decider—The Origin." ("How did he become the Decider? Has he always been the Decider?") The *Huffington Post* set Bush's quote to the tune of "I Am the Walrus," by the Beatles, and the phrase "the decider" soon became nearly ubiquitous in the media. (It was the focus of at least three stories in the *New York Times* in 2006 and was mentioned many times more than that.) Today, entering "the decider" into Google returns more than a million results, ranging from references to one of Bill Maher's comedy specials to a *Time* magazine cover story on Anthony Kennedy ("From Gay Marriage to Obamacare, Justice Anthony Kennedy Is the Decider") to a comparison of the wide receivers Sammy Watkins and Mike Evans. What is remarkable is how much of this can be traced directly to Bush's comment. Between January 1, 1851, and April 17, 2006—that is, over a period of 155 years—the *New York Times* used the expression "the decider" only nine times, which works out to roughly once every seventeen years. In the eight years since Bush's press conference, however, it has appeared in the paper 493 times. That's five times a month.

What is going on here? Several things, I suspect. The locution "the decider" sounds odd—as one retired linguistics professor notes in an amusingly annoyed blog commentary, "No normal person would ever utter such a thing." But peculiarity can't entirely explain our response—for one thing,

President Bush said many things far quirkier. (For sheer strangeness, it would be hard to top "I know the human being and fish can coexist peacefully.") More important, I think, is that something about "the decider" seems childish, or rather child*like*. "I'm the decider, and I decide what is best": This seems to capture the hunger for control that is characteristic of all humans but that is completely unmasked in three-year-olds. Control means getting to decide when bedtime will be, or which shoes will be worn, or whether lollipops will be forthcoming. Control, to a three-year-old, means owning the choice. And this seems amusing because as adults we realize, albeit unconsciously, exactly how doubtful that ownership must always be, and how delicate a contrivance lies at the center of our sense of possession.

———

ONE OF THE LESS REMARKED features of "The Road Not Taken" is that it offers a portrait not just of decisions but of deciders—or, to pick a more helpful word, of selves. This shouldn't be surprising, considering that the poem is routinely brought out for occasions that are supposed to mark milestones in our personal development: graduations, retirement parties, vow renewals, lifetime achievement ceremonies. In these instances, "The Road Not Taken" is meant to celebrate *us*, not any particular handful of individual decisions. As the ninety thousandth high school valedictorian declaims the poem's final stanza, everyone in the audience understands that they are being encouraged not simply to continue picking less traveled roads, but to aspire to a certain kind of glorified personhood.

That personhood is, above all else, *authentic*. "Two roads diverged in a wood, and I— / I took the one less traveled by": The claim here, according to the poem's popular interpretation, is that the speaker took the more arduous spiritual and personal journey. This is also, not at all coincidentally, the path to the truest version of the speaker's self, according to most models of self-improvement. Indeed, if "The Road Not Taken" can serve as a metaphor for thirty years of behavioral economics, psychology, and neuroscience, it is at least equally emblematic of the half-century-old self-help movement, as its popularity in motivational posters can attest.

This is in part traceable to a single book. In 1978, M. Scott Peck published *The Road Less Traveled: A New Psychology of Love, Traditional Values and Spiritual Growth*, a guide to reforming oneself that drew heavily on Peck's career as a psychiatrist and his somewhat unconventional religious views. (His final book, published in 2005, was a memoir about exorcisms.) *The Road Less Traveled* languished for several years, but by the early eighties, word of mouth and Peck's assiduous courting of reviewers had turned it into one of the foundational texts of modern self-help. In a

2012 article, the *Christian Science Monitor* declared it to be among the ten greatest self-improvement books ever written (placing it in company with those of Benjamin Franklin and Dale Carnegie), and according to Peck's website, *The Road Less Traveled* "has sold over 7 million copies and remained on the *New York Times* Best Seller List longer than any other paperback book." As with many self-help guides, the book itself is a kind of olive loaf composed of corn-fed common sense ("The process of listening to children differs depending on the age of the child") liberally seasoned with nuggets of kookiness ("Moreover, were I ever to have a case in which I concluded after careful and judicious consideration that my patient's spiritual growth would be substantially furthered by our having sexual relations, I would proceed to have them").

Outside of its title, *The Road Less Traveled* never mentions the poem from which it takes its name. But Peck's reading of Frost is probably even stronger for being implicit. "Life is difficult," begins *The Road Less Traveled*, and you can tell Peck means it, because he gives those three words their very own paragraph. What we need to learn, he goes on to argue, is self-discipline. This will allow us to see that "the fact that life is difficult no longer matters." Later, we will discover that in order to follow "the road of spiritual growth," we must "begin by distrusting what we already believe, by actively seeking the threatening and unfamiliar." The book is essentially a three-hundred-page elaboration of the message most people attribute to "The Road Not Taken": Life is a hard, lonely, but ultimately triumphant struggle.

This has become a popular idea—a very, very popular idea. The self-improvement market, which includes books, seminars, "life coaches," motivational speakers, and so forth, is now generally estimated at twelve billion dollars a year in the United States alone. (Self-help is "predominantly an American phenomenon," as *City Journal* puts it.) There are in the ballpark of fifty thousand self-improvement books in print, and each year another three or four thousand new titles embark upon a massive salmon run up the guru's mountain. That's a lot of money to choose to pay, and a lot of books to choose to buy, all in order to become "the decider."

But who, exactly, is doing the deciding? It can be hard to tell from self-help publications, which tend to mingle as many as half a dozen notions about the selves they are intending to assist. This confusion is to be expected. Self-help takes its cues from the day-to-day ideas about selfhood that persist among ordinary people, and those ideas are either complex or irretrievably muddled, depending upon how you look at them. In general, though, they tend to fall under the umbrella of one of two overarching metaphors: "self-creation" and "self-discovery." The first metaphor, "creation," suggests that the self is something we can improve, or even build from scratch, much in the way we might start or enhance a business. When people want to invoke this aspect of the self, they say things like "I need to choose who I want to be" or "We are the sum of our choices." In fact, "We are the sum of our choices" is such an attractively responsible-sounding phrase that it has been repeated nearly verbatim in, among many other examples, movies like *I Think I Love My Wife* (in which it is deployed with maximum earnestness by Chris Rock), *X-Men: Days of Future Past* (James McAvoy, playing Professor X, wields the earnestness), Woody Allen's *Crimes and Misdemeanors* (earnestness by actual psychologist Martin Bergmann), and of course roughly ten thousand self-improvement/motivational books and websites, where it is often credited to the legendary guru Wayne Dyer, author of the 33-million-copy-selling *Your Erroneous Zones*.

The second metaphor—"discovery"—suggests that the self isn't made or shaped, but rather is uncovered through hard archaeological work, like an Etruscan vase or the tomb of Tutankhamen. This self isn't created—it is revealed and expressed. When people have this view of the self in mind, they say things like "I've got to figure out who I am" or "I wanted to say what I was all about." This way of thinking is an equally powerful force in contemporary culture, and it appears in everything from the songs of Macklemore ("I had to find out who I really was," he declares in "Make the Money") to the wisdom of Eleanor Roosevelt ("I think that somehow, we learn who we really are"). The idea that the self is "found" or "discovered" usually includes the suggestion that the self is constant and solid—almost a substance, like gold or myrrh. "Uncover the treasure of your true self," advises the self-help author Guy Finley, because "you have been left a great inheritance." At the end of the road less traveled, it would appear, is a big sack of loot.

The difficulty is that if the self is something we make (like a business), it's hard to see how it can also be something we find (like a chest of doubloons). The metaphors are in considerable tension, if not contradictory. Do we take the less traveled road because doing so will reveal the glitter of the True Self? Or do we take that road because doing so somehow creates the True Self? What is interesting is that people seem generally happy to ignore this tension, shifting frictionlessly from one model of selfhood to the other, sometimes within the same sentence. If Wayne Dyer tells us that we are the sum of our choices, he is also perfectly willing to say that "letting the ego-illusion become your identity can prevent you from knowing your true self." So we are the sum of our choices, but there is also some "true self" that remains hidden. By the same token, while one hates to pick on Eleanor Roosevelt, I should point out that when I quoted her earlier saying "we learn who we really are," I could have added that she immediately followed that remark with "and then live with that decision." So we find our essence by . . . deciding what it is? She also asserts that "we shape our lives and we shape ourselves. The process never ends until we die." Can I "really" be something that I am also choosing? And if so, who (or what) is this "I" person?

NOT ROBERT FROST, least of all in "The Road Not Taken." "I have written," said Frost in a letter to Sidney Cox, "to keep the curious out of the secret places of my mind both in my verse and in my letters to such as you. A subject has to be held outside of me with struts and as it were set up for an object." And in a letter to Robert Newdick: "The point I was trying to make is that I was a very hard person to make out if I was any judge of human nature. I might easily be most deceiving when most bent on telling the truth." Frost is talking in both letters about the misconceptions of biographers (and readers), but he plainly savors the idea of being a mystery to himself as well. "I was a very hard person to make out if I was any judge of human nature": Who is the "I" here? Wouldn't Frost know whether or not he was "any judge of human nature"? And why is the sentence in the past tense? Likewise, why say you "might" be most deceiving when trying hardest to be truthful? Can't you just be truthful? As with his attitude toward his own choices (or lack thereof), Frost's view of his own inner life was a combination of indomitable certainty and serene ignorance. His public showmanship mirrored a private theater in which the ultimate question was not the authenticity of the performer but the canniness of the drama and the allure of the masks.

"The Road Not Taken" is a series of such masks. Though the poem is (to an extent) about Edward Thomas, the "I" of the poem isn't purely Thomas any more than the "I" of, say, "Stopping by Woods on a Snowy Evening" is Frost. Rather, Frost gives us a speaker whose identity—whose self—is an interplay of questions about personhood. As the poem progresses, these questions emerge in the uncertain ground between the poem's popular interpretation and its more critically acceptable reading. The former imagines a self that is unified and authentic—a self that has chosen the less traveled road to emerge in its full splendor. The latter presupposes a fragmentary, improvisational sort of self that is unsure of its own choices, aware of its tendency to invent explanations for events over which it has no control, and skeptical of its future stability.

In keeping with his usual habits, Frost provides support for both positions, and potential responses for nearly all questions that anyone might ask. Consider the poem's second and third lines:

And sorry I could not travel both
And be one traveler . . .

As I said in "The Poem," these lines imply that we are changed by the choices we make. (Frost underscores this potential reading a few lines later when he claims, "I doubted if I should ever come back.") So the suggestion, it would appear, is that the self is created. And yet if we take the lines even more literally, we can get another curious angle on the self, although it involves a slightly baroque thought experiment. Imagine that as he ponders the roads, the speaker tries to travel both by undergoing a fission process that will send half of his brain down one road and half down the other, without causing him any permanent harm. He does so, and each brain hemisphere proceeds down one branch of the fork. But because "I could not travel both / And be one traveler"—that is, one "I"—the self doesn't survive the process. Either it's attached to one of the travelers or it has been destroyed. The implication here is that the self possesses an unsplittable core that makes us *us*.

This may seem like too much meaning to extract from nine words. Even the best poets have bad moments, and it's tempting to suppose that in writing this odd description from which so many peculiar meanings can be drawn, Frost might simply have been clumsy. It's possible, of course. But the appearance of clumsiness is rarely to be trusted in a writer so eager to be underestimated, and in this case it's a judgment to be especially wary of. In a letter from 1912 to

Susan Hayes Ward, one of his few early supporters, Frost wrote of walking down a country lane as it approached a crossroads and meeting

> a man, who to my own unfamiliar eyes and in the dusk looked for all the world like myself, coming down the other, his approach to the point where our paths must intersect being so timed that unless one of us pulled up we must inevitably collide. I felt as if I was going to meet my own image in a slanting mirror. Or say I felt as we slowly converged on the same point with the same noiseless yet laborious stride as if we were two images about to float together with the un-crossing of someone's eyes. I verily expected to take up or absorb this other self and feel the stronger by the addition for the three-mile journey home.

Critics generally consider this episode one of the inspirations for "The Road Not Taken" ("neither is much travelled," Frost wrote of the two crossing paths), and it foregrounds the extent to which Frost was thinking about the fragile device of the self—the way it can seem multiple, malleable ("to take up or absorb this other self"), simultaneously who we are now, who we were, and who we might become.

As usual, Frost forecloses no options. Consider the famous last stanza:

I shall be telling this with a sigh
Somewhere ages and ages hence:
Two roads diverged in a wood, and I—
I took the one less traveled by,
And that has made all the difference.

Notice how Frost repeats the word "I" from the end of the third line to the beginning of the fourth: "and I— / I . . ." He could just as easily have written, "Two roads diverged in a wood, and I / Walked down the one less traveled by" or "Two roads diverged in a wood, and I / Pursued the one less traveled by." But he didn't. Instead he inserted a pause as the "I" shifts to another "I." The pause is a signal. It suggests, among other things, uncertainty—uncertainty that a choice has been made, yes, but also uncertainty regarding the "I" that is being asked to fill the gap between the choice in question and the projected future. Do we think that the speaker repeats the "I" because, after a moment's consideration, he's confident his future self will believe he is the same "I" as his choosing self? Or does he repeat it to emphasize the potential difference between the two? I suggested earlier that we should be wary of assuming that the speaker is accurately anticipating his mental state. In fact, a number of psychological studies have demonstrated that we're generally fairly bad at predicting how we'll feel about a given set of future conditions (this is known as affective or hedonic forecasting), and it's fair to wonder if our ignorance about our own emotions might arise from uncertainty about our continuing identity.

The poem's much-quoted final line is equally ambiguous. Why, after all, say that the choice has made "all the difference," a phrase that bordered on cliché even in Frost's era? Why not say something equally banal but more definitive, like "And that has led to my success"? Why use a comparative term, "difference," instead of a straightforward description, like "triumph"? Three explanations make sense here, all of which allow Frost to expand the scope of his ending. The first is that the phrase "all the difference" allows Frost to raise questions about the extent of the "difference" at issue—"all the difference" could mean "a great deal of difference," but it could also mean "no difference whatsoever." (He would certainly have been aware of—and happy to play upon—the related idiom "all the difference it made," as in this sentence from *Anne of Green Gables*: "Anne washed her hair, scrubbing it vigorously with soap and water, but for all the difference it made she might as well have been scouring its original red.") Second, the word "difference" is neutral with respect to outcome, which lets Frost invoke the full range of possible "different" futures for his speaker. (For all we know, the speaker's life has spiraled rapidly downhill since his choice.) Finally, "all the difference" implies a prepositional phrase: The choice makes "all the difference" *in* or *to* something or someone. The poem's popular interpretation assumes that the speaker's life is what has been changed, but the speaker's self is at least as good a candidate. After all, we've just been presented with a densely knotted scenario in which the speaker's current self is imagining a future self that is speculating on the notion of "difference," while gratuitously repeating the word "I." The result is a tangle of memory, sense impressions, guesswork, and storytelling.

———

WHICH, AS IT TURNS OUT, is a fair summary of modern perspectives on the self. Those perspectives are legion. But they may be grouped along a continuum that stretches, on one end, from the idea that the self is a unified, persistent entity with describable properties (almost like the heart) to, on the other end, the notion that the self is just a passing sensation of connectedness that we mistakenly equate with genuine wholeness and/or continuity. As you may have noticed, these two extremes loosely correspond with the everyday notions of a self that is "found" (as unified entities can be) and a self that is "constructed" (as concepts derived from passing sensations always are). That's probably no coincidence. The self is a deeply personal phenomenon—the most personal phenomenon of all—and as such, one might expect its scholarly discussion to track its commonplace conception more closely than in, say, the case of quantum mechanics. Our evidence for views on the self is unavoidably entangled with the subjectivity of actual people.

The view of the self as a unified, continuous entity is identified historically with a parade of thinkers extending from Plato through Descartes and Kant. It's fallen on hard times in recent years, however, so when it emerges, it tends to do so through the back door of arguments on related topics like free will. Here is the philosopher Susan Wolf, writing on that very question and referring to the views of several other philosophers with whom she largely agrees:

> If we are responsible agents, it is not just because our actions are within the control of our wills, but because, in addition, our wills are not just psychological states *in* us, but expressions of characters that come *from* us. . . . The key to responsibility lies in the fact that responsible agents are those for whom it is . . . the case that their wills are within the control of their *selves* in some deeper sense.

"Their *selves* in some deeper sense": To have a "deep self" is presumably to have more than just a bare handful of sensory impressions and some ephemeral sense of wholeness. If this sort of self isn't quite what Descartes had in mind, it's still robust enough to be counted toward the "unified" side of the spectrum.

It's much easier these days to find philosophers, psychologists, and scientists willing to say that the self is fragmentary, or even an illusion (though one always wonders: an illusion to whom?). This point of view owes a debt to the eighteenth-century Scottish philosopher David Hume, who provided what remains the most pointed argument against the self's unity. "There are some philosophers," he wrote in 1739, "who imagine we are every moment intimately conscious of what we call our SELF; that we feel its existence and its continuance in existence; and are certain, beyond the evidence of a demonstration, both of its perfect identity and simplicity." Hume continues in high Scots dudgeon:

> I may venture to affirm of the rest of mankind, that they are nothing but a bundle or collection of different perceptions, which succeed each other with an inconceivable rapidity, and are in a perpetual flux and movement. Our eyes cannot turn in their sockets without varying our perceptions. Our thought is still more variable than our sight; and all our other senses and faculties contribute to this change; nor is there any single power of the soul, which remains unalterably the same, perhaps for one moment. The mind is a

kind of theatre, where several perceptions successively make their appearance; pass, re-pass, glide away, and mingle in an infinite variety of postures and situations. There is properly no simplicity in it at one time, nor identity in different; whatever natural propension we may have to imagine that simplicity and identity.

The "bundle theory," as it's sometimes called, has become increasingly attractive as science has steadily whittled away at the idea of the core self. The philosopher Derek Parfit, for example, has argued that we have no self at all, but merely an overlapping succession of mental states—a variation on Hume's theory that has become moderately famous, in that it is perhaps the only philosophical conception of personal identity to be extensively discussed in *The New Yorker*. What is particularly interesting, though, is Parfit's description of his personal reaction to the realization that he didn't need a unified self. That response appears in a section of his (massive) treatise *Reasons and Persons* titled "Liberation from the Self":

Is the truth depressing? Some may find it so. But I find it liberating, and consoling. When I believed that my existence was such a further fact, I seemed imprisoned in myself. My life seemed like a glass tunnel, through which I was moving faster every year, and at the end of which there was darkness. When I changed my view, the walls of my glass tunnel disappeared. I now live in the open air. There is still a difference between my life and the lives of other people. But the difference is less. . . . I am less concerned about the rest of my own life, and more concerned about the lives of others.

In the yellow wood, he has seen the roads diverge, each inclining, as Frost once put it, toward "black and utter chaos," and realized that there is really no "I" to feel trapped and fearful. That is a good thing, to be sure. And yet the primary attraction of this passage isn't its logic, but the throb of emotion that propels its lines into arcs of metaphor ("My life seemed like a glass tunnel," "I now live in the open air"). One hears in these oddly poignant statements not the impersonal sound of the self being diminished, but the familiar music of a particular self being transformed.

But what exactly is being changed? One of the problems with the self—whether modeled by Frost or theorized by neuroscientists—is definitional. When we say "the self," are we talking about a self-conception? Consciousness? A kind of personal narrative? There is a tendency, even among the most careful thinkers, to overlook the fact that when the average person talks in a way that implicates the self, that person often says things that seem to refer to very different aspects of identity. For instance:

- *I don't feel like myself today.*
- *There I am!* [while looking at photos from childhood]
- *Yes, I moved your coffee cup.*

These are all ways of invoking an "I," and yet they seem only lightly tethered to one another. Is the "I" who moves a coffee cup really the same "I" who appears in a thirty-year-old picture? And if not, does it make sense to call them both "the self"?

One of the most helpful recent answers to these questions appears in a collection of essays called *Self to Self*, by the philosopher J. David Velleman. Velleman denies that there is a single entity that corresponds to all of the ways in which we think and talk about our selves. Instead, the so-called self is really a set of "reflexive guises" that correspond to "at least three distinct selves." (By "reflexive" he means that the way of thinking in question takes itself as its own subject, as in the sentence "I look at myself," in which what "I" am looking at is "me.") The three aspects of selfhood that Velleman has in mind roughly correspond to the sentences above. They are:

A person's self-image. This is how a person describes who he is and what he stands for. As Velleman puts it, "It is like a photograph in the subject's mental album, showing just another person but bearing on the reverse side 'This is me.'" This is the self that prompts us to say things like "That job just didn't feel like who I am."

Self-sameness through time. This is "the relation that connects a person to his past and future selves, as they are called." Velleman believes that such selves are "the past and future persons whom the subject can identify as the 'I' of a memory or the 'I' of a plan." This is the self that lets us see ourselves in old VHS tapes of our tenth birthday party.

Autonomous agency. This self is "the agent's faculty of causal understanding"—the way a person distinguishes between things that are in some sense genuinely his doing and things that are not. Snoring while asleep is not your action in the same way that, for instance, buying tickets to see Iron Maiden because you really enjoy Bruce Dickinson's singing would be. This self says, "I am doing this because I have this preference."

As you can see, these are very different functions, and considering them as arising from different aspects of selfhood helps smooth over some of the problems that arise from treating them as unified.

There are surely difficulties with this conception, as there are with all models of selfhood. But it's interesting to see how the division of the self into three parts manages to accommodate the tangle of identity in "The Road Not Taken." We have the "I" who thinks one road should be preferred because it seems "less traveled"—this establishes the speaker's self-image as a person who favors solitary paths. Then we have the present self projecting into the future ("I shall be telling this with a sigh / Somewhere ages and ages hence"). And of course, we have the actual taking of the road, which Frost nicely complicates by making it unclear whether the speaker succeeded in explaining his choice to himself as something that arose from a cause. (The roads are, after all, "about the same.") Perhaps what waits at the end of the road isn't the authentic self, or a bundle of impressions, but a federation.

———

BUT IF SO, it is a federation without neighboring states. The chooser is alone in "The Road Not Taken," and the drama of the self unfolds in private. That privacy is somewhat surprising, given the poem's supposed origin in the long walks Frost once took with Edward Thomas. Remember that Frost repeatedly claimed that he wrote "The Road Not Taken" as a way of gently teasing Thomas for his habit of reproaching himself for failing to take a path that might have led to more interesting scenery. But if Thomas regretted his choices in this way, it seems important to acknowledge that he did so because he wanted to show the passed-up scenery *to Frost*. The great significance of their walks was the companionship that these two men—each possessing a vast and idiosyncratic intelligence, and no longer young—found in their time together. It seems strange that one of the greatest intimacies of Frost's life would become the source for a poem from which he appears to have excised his own role.

And yet, considered at the proper angle, it makes perfect sense. One of the strongest themes in Frost's life and work is his belief in personal agency, whether conscious or (as he once put it) by "accidents on purpose." Among American poets, he is the great individualist, to whom all connotations of that heavily freighted description fully apply. Consider this excerpt from *The Paris Review*'s interview with Frost in 1960, less than three years before his death:

INTERVIEWER: Your best friend in those years was Edward Thomas?

FROST: Yes—quite separate again from everybody his age. He was as isolated as I was. Nobody knew he wrote poetry. He didn't write poetry until he started to war, and that had something to do with my life with him. We got to be great friends. No, I had an instinct against belonging to any of those crowds. I've had friends, but very scat-

tering, a scattering over there. You know, I could have . . .
Pound had an afternoon meeting once a week with Flint
and Aldington and H. D. and at one time Hulme, I think.
Hulme started with them. They met every week to re-
write each other's poems.

INTERVIEWER: You saw Hulme occasionally? Was it at these
rewriting sessions, or didn't you bother with them?

FROST: Yes, I knew Hulme, knew him quite well. But I never
went to one of those meetings. I said to Pound, "What do
you do?" He said, "Rewrite each other's poems." And I
said, "Why?" He said, "To squeeze the water out of them."
"That sounds like a parlor game to me," I said, "and I'm
a serious artist"—kidding, you know. And he laughed
and he didn't invite me any more.

One sees every side of Frost's individualism here: the barely
concealed loneliness ("as isolated as I was"), the simmering
pride ("I had an instinct against belonging to any of those
crowds"), the contempt for those with less faith in their own
standards ("'That sounds like a parlor game to me,' I said").
"The Road Not Taken" may well have begun as a joke, but as
it became a poem—as it began "to brave alien entangle-
ments," as Frost would say—it took on the rocky demeanor
of its maker. Two friends—"He was as isolated as I was"—
became one chooser, whether by merger or separation.

The model of the self that results is particularly, though not exclusively, American. Whether the average person in the United States talks about the self as being "created" or "found" or both, that person generally has in mind a self that is oriented toward, well, itself. That is, we assume that selves are strongly centered in individual people; that they are, in fact, what helps make those people individuals in the first place. For the past three decades, cross-cultural psychologists have been studying the ways in which different societies approach questions of agency, choice, and self-construction. The consensus holds that societies that are inclined toward individualism—the United States is usually considered the exemplar—tend to produce people whose self-conceptions depend on precisely this strong separation between themselves and others. The Western "I," according to this view, takes itself as "the ultimate reference point," as the social psychologist Sheena Iyengar puts it, or "the decider," as George W. Bush would have it. This model is sometimes referred to as the "independent self."

But there is another way to look at things. More collectivist societies tend to produce people whose views of their selves are more heavily influenced (and to an extent determined) by their social relations. This model is often referred to as the "interdependent self." Very broadly speaking, the interdependent self is less conscious of boundaries between itself and others, more willing to perceive actions as occur-

.ring because of group dynamics (rather than assertions of solitary will), less interested in choices being perceived as individual, and more conscious of the thoughts and feelings of other people from the same cultural group. This doesn't mean that an interdependent self is automatically favorably inclined toward the people with whom it has relationships, merely that such a self will be more aware of and responsive to those relationships. Or, to put it another way, the interdependent self is perfectly capable of being annoyed with its siblings; it's just going to think of itself as being implicated in the lives of those siblings more often and more deeply than its independent counterpart.

The differences between these two general ideas of self-hood have emerged in a series of psychological experiments dating back to a foundational study by Hazel Rose Markus and Shinobu Kitayama in 1991. Researchers following in the footsteps of Markus and Kitayama have found, for example, that when offered five pens, only one of which is colored differently from the others, almost 80 percent of European Americans will pick the distinctive pen, as opposed to roughly 30 percent of East Asians. Similar distinctions emerge in research regarding the ways the accomplishments of a given self are thought to have been achieved. A study of coverage of the 2000 and 2002 Olympics found that the American media focused to a much higher degree on "the positive personal characteristics of athletes and on the competition"—in other words, the assumption was that athletes had been successful because of their individual will to compete, not because of the intervention of others. Japanese coverage, by contrast, tended to emphasize "a broader array of factors, both positive and negative," with the athletes' backgrounds and experiences generally appearing more often than references to competition. A second part of that study involved giving subjects in the United States and Japan a biographical sketch of a fictional Olympic athlete from their respective countries. The researchers asked the subjects to pick the most relevant items for media coverage of that athlete from a list of forty that had been taken from actual news reports. As the study puts it:

> The Americans chose statements emphasizing two categories—personal attributes and uniqueness— significantly more than the Japanese. The Japanese, however, chose statements emphasizing four categories—athlete's coach and team, motivation, emotion, and doubt—significantly more than the Americans.

"Personal attributes and uniqueness" are the hallmarks of the American who has taken the less traveled road, whether in a poem or on a podium. After all, no matter what one thinks is the primary meaning of "The Road Not Taken," it's hard to miss the fact that there are no other people in it. Even in the closing stanza, when the speaker announces "I shall be telling this," he never says to whom he'll be doing the telling. It seems as likely as anything else that he'll be talking to himself, like an authentic American.

That said, categories like "independent" and "interdependent" are obviously crude tools with which to measure the fine-grained material of the human self, and as such, they should be taken to suggest only very loose general tendencies in societies—the point of cross-cultural psychology isn't to imply that Americans are from Mars, while the Japanese are from Venus. A person from an East Asian country might be extraordinarily independent, just as an American might be strongly collectively oriented. In addition, someone who is placed in a situation that doesn't fit the usual circumstances of his culture may quickly take on the assumptions of the new environment. For instance, a study of Korean American students who were spending the summer in Korea indicated that after only five weeks, they were beginning to respond in ways more typical of the surrounding culture (which, unlike American culture, is generally considered to involve an interdependent self-construction). Researchers have even been able to evoke a more independent or interdependent response from bicultural subjects like Chinese Americans simply by showing them well-known icons such as the Statue of Liberty beforehand, or by asking them to respond to questions in Chinese instead of English (a tactic referred to as cultural priming).

Moreover, even within the overarching idea of the extravagantly autonomous American self, there are many shades of individualism. The anthropologist Adrie Kusserow has suggested that the kind of individualism found among lower- and working-class American communities differs sharply from that found in middle-class settings. She characterizes the distinction as "hard" (that is, the self develops strong edges that serve as walls or weapons) versus "soft" (the self is figured as unfolding or flowering) and also notes that these formations can have an offensive or defensive tilt. Her description of the language used by the upper-working-class mothers of a neighborhood in Queens is worth pausing over (emphases mine):

Mothers wove phrases such as "try things out," "get a lot more out of this world," "break away," "go for your dreams," and "*the road less traveled*" into their general discourse on the importance of being self-determined, persevering, self-confident, and courageous—really "going for it" because "the sky's the limit." For them,

progress would not be a delicate process, nor would the
parents constantly be there to help the child emerge.

It would be hard to imagine a better description of the indi-
vidualism of Frost himself, whose own background would
have made him strongly sympathetic to the women in ques-
tion. It's not a joke or trick that his poem would now serve as
a governing metaphor for their ambitions. Frost was aware of
the ambiguities of choice and self-reliance, certainly, but
that didn't make him any less sure that we are the primary
engineers of our separate fates.

It is a way of looking at the world that is hard to avoid in
the United States. It frames the American self-help industry,
with its relentless focus on a self that improves or grows be-
cause an individual has elected to *do something* ("It's the
choice to show up and be real," says Brené Brown), rather
than because a community has come together to help one of
its troubled members. It is unavoidable in the advertising
industry, which is a 180-billion-dollar business in the United
States—more than a third of the global total. "Be yourself,"
advises Audi America in marketing the Q5 crossover SUV
while dozens of nearly identical beige cars made by Audi's
competitors roll by and a background song advises us to
"find one that don't look the same." German advertising for
the same car involves a series of thousands of placards being
flipped precisely by a crowd of hundreds, and Japanese ads

make a whimsical visual joke with a bicycle. If you're selling something in the United States, so the thinking goes, you had better play to customers' desire to differentiate themselves. The historical pedigree of that desire extends to the country's founding. "Without the possibility of choice and the exercise of choice," said Thomas Jefferson, "a man is not a man, but a member, an instrument, a thing." *A member, an instrument, a thing.* It is against this backdrop that the independent American self is built and claimed, for better and worse. It is against this backdrop that the crossroads emerges, with the solitary chooser at its center.

The Crossroads

T he Road Not Taken" is a portrait of the choosing self. But it's also a critique of that self—and in this sense, the path the speaker eventually takes is less important than the structure of the crossroads on which he stands. On one branch of the diverging road, we have the celebratory individualism of Ralph Waldo Emerson: "Whoso would be a man must be a nonconformist." On the other branch, we have the skepticism of Tocqueville, who worries that Americans believe they

> owe nothing to any man, they expect nothing from any man; they acquire the habit of always considering themselves as standing alone, and they are apt to imagine that their whole destiny is in their own hands.
>
> Thus not only does democracy make every man forget his ancestors, but it hides his descendants, and separates his contemporaries from him; it throws him

back forever upon himself alone, and threatens in the end to confine him entirely within the solitude of his own heart.

In the middle of these visions, perpetually choosing and returning, we find a speaker who is attracted to less traveled roads but unsure of his choice, uncertain of his continuity, uncomforted by a future that may or may not even be "different." We see the double that Frost envisioned walking toward him in 1912 ("my own image in a slanting mirror"), and we see the twinned figures of Frost and Edward Thomas, approaching the roads that would lead one of them to death in a futile war, the other to a career as the most famous poet of his era. We see the place of judgment and redemption described in one of America's iconic songs, Robert Johnson's "Cross Road Blues":

> *I went to the crossroad, fell down on my knees.*
> *I went to the crossroad, fell down on my knees.*
> *Asked the Lord above, "Have mercy, save poor*
> *   Bob, if you please."*

We see the roads that will make all the difference, the roads that lead to more of the same, and the roads that lead only to other roads.

But most of all, we see the centrality of the junction itself. "The Road Not Taken" never mentions what the speaker finds on the path he eventually takes; instead, the poem concludes by echoing its own opening line, "Two roads diverged in a wood," as if to return us to the forest in which we started. What matters most, the poem suggests, is the dilemma of the crossroads.

That dilemma has a long-standing part in the Western tradition. In *Robert Frost Among His Poems*, Jeffrey S. Cramer provides a helpful compilation of examples of "the 'two roads' theme," as he puts it, that Frost would likely have had in mind when writing "The Road Not Taken." These include, among others, the *Aeneid* ("Here is the place / Where the road forks"), Henry Wadsworth Longfellow ("by turning down this street instead of the other, we may let slip some great occasion of good"), Emily Dickinson ("Our feet were almost come / To that odd fork in Being's road"), and Frost's favorite philosopher, William James ("only one [of two roads], and that one either one, shall be chosen"). To this we could add the prophet Ezekiel's vision of the fall of Jerusalem: "For the king of Babylon stands at the parting of the way, at the fork in the two roads, to use divination; he shakes the arrows, he consults the teraphim, he inspects the liver." And in *Oedipus the King*, first performed almost twenty-five hundred years ago, Sophocles gives us an especially relevant demonstration of the crossroad's symbolic resonance:

OEDIPUS: I thought I heard you say that Laius was cut down at a place where three roads meet.

JOCASTA: That was the story. It hasn't died out yet.

OEDIPUS: Where did this thing happen? Be precise.

JOCASTA: A place called Phocis, where two branching roads, one from Daulia, one from Delphi, come together—a crossroads.

The crossroads is where Oedipus, unaware, determines his fate by killing his own father—unless, of course, that fate has already been determined for him in advance by some greater power. (In this sense and in several others, the overlap between "The Road Not Taken" and *Oedipus the King* is considerable.) But before Oedipus makes the choice to attack Laius, he's neither a king nor a patricide, nor even the person he believes himself to be, since he's spent his life up to that point assuming he was the son of the wrong man. Before he makes the choice, he's nothing and anything. He is, you might say, pure potential.

This pause—this brief moment between question and answer—is the essence of a crossroads. At the intersection of roads A, B, and C is a space that is simultaneously all roads and none; it's the deep breath before a journey can be undertaken, or a transition completed. In a series of essays beginning in *The Forest of Symbols,* in 1967, the anthropologist Victor Turner outlined a concept called "liminality," which he originally applied to ritual processes in Central Africa but later used much more broadly. Here is how Turner describes the idea in "Variations on a Theme of Liminality":

> Let us refer to the state and process of mid-transition as "liminality" and consider a few of its very odd properties. Those undergoing it—call them "liminaries"—are betwixt-and-between established states of politico-jural structure. They evade ordinary cognitive classification too, for they are neither-this-nor-that, here-nor-there, one-thing-not-the-other. Out of their mundane structural context, they are in a sense "dead" to the world, and liminality has many symbols of death. . . . But the most characteristic midliminal symbolism is that of paradox, or being both this and that.

A crossroads gives us exactly this scenario. The person who stands in such a place, debating his path, is neither on one road nor on the other: He is literally betwixt and between. This is why, in Frost's poetry, the liminal is not just a space for "symbols of death" or "paradox," but a space for performance and metaphor, the great engines of his poetry. A person who is playing a role both is and isn't the role played. A metaphor joins two terms so that they both are and aren't each other. The crossroads is, as Frost would say, the only spot in which one actually *can* travel both roads as one traveler.

This is why the crossroads has always been where one ventures in order to blur or merge things that are defined in opposition to each other. It is the place for that which has no place. And as such, it's never quite to be trusted. In ancient Greece, for example, crossroads were often marked with statues or shrines dedicated to the goddess Hecate. These emblems, called *hekataia*, typically depicted Hecate with three faces, each pointing toward one of the branching roads, and citizens would leave offerings at them to seek the goddess's aid in passage from one place to another. But as the scholar S. I. Johnson explains, the Greeks would also bring "the polluted remains of household purification rituals" to the crossroads to be disposed of. This was because, as Johnson writes,

Both types [of worship] ultimately grew from the liminal nature of crossroads, but in opposing ways. On the one hand, crossroads were uncertain, dissociated places of passage, where protective actions were necessary. On the other hand, by the very fact of their dissociation, they were convenient vacuums into which ancient man could dispose of his religious and societal refuse—or call up that refuse, in the form of restless souls, to aid him in the performance of magic.

We want strength to face the crossroads (whether from an ancient goddess or our own inner fortitude), but we also use the crossroads to contain or summon the troubling, the uncertain, the uncanny. It lies both outside and inside the expected order of things. It belongs to no one and everyone.

As do Robert Frost and "The Road Not Taken." Frost is the great poet of the liminal, and his natural terrain is the unsettled intersection of opposing paths. "All the fun," he wrote to Louis Untermeyer, "is outside saying things that suggest formulae that won't formulate—that almost but don't quite formulate. I should like to be so subtle at this game as to seem to the casual person altogether obvious." In another letter to Untermeyer, Frost begins by proclaiming himself "orthodox" and in opposition to "mad glad stuff," but this train of thought rapidly gives way to a vision of the uncanny disturbance at the core of his own practice:

The conviction closes in on me that I was cast for gloom as the sparks fly upward, I was about to say: I am of deep shadow all compact like onion within onion and the savor of me is oil of tears. I have heard laughter by daylight when I thought it was my own because at that moment when it broke I had parted my lips to take food. Just so I have been afraid of myself and caught at my throat when I thought I was making some terrible din of a mill whistle that happened to come on the same instant with the opening of my mouth to yawn. But I have not laughed. No man can tell you the sound or the way of my laughter. I have neighed at night in the woods behind a house like vampires. But there are no vampires there are no ghouls there are no demons, there is no nothing but me.

"There is no nothing but me" at the crossroads, where a mouth opens without a reliable connection to the "I" that should govern it, and where the mind turns to the rise of the dead and the monstrous. It's the kind of place where one would need a guide, though if he is Robert Frost, he will "only [have] at heart your getting lost," as he writes in "Directive."

It may seem odd for such a liminal figure to have become so thoroughly equated with a country often considered central to world affairs, whose leaders regularly refer to it as "the indispensable nation." But the importance of the crossroads—and the poets and gods of the crossroads—is that they allow us to change, to escape, to emerge or disappear. In this sense, the United States is, perhaps above all else, a liminal territory. ("Is anything central?" asks John Ashbery in "The One Thing That Can Save America.") When we think of Japan, we think of Mount Fuji; when we think of France, we think of the Eiffel Tower. Russia evokes the Winter Palace, India the Taj Mahal. But when we think of the United States, we see the Statue of Liberty: the sculpture that marks the threshold, the *limen*, as the Romans would have said. America, alone among nations, has as its most recognized symbol not one of its great buildings or natural features, but an invocation of its doorway. And a doorway, like a crossroads, is neither here nor there; it is a possibility. In the case of the Statue of Liberty, the doorway is even more striking because it was called forth not by the sculpture's original conception (its designer, Frédéric Auguste Bartholdi, intended the figure to signify liberty shining outward from the United States to the rest of the world) but by a feature it acquired seventeen years after its October 1886 dedication. That feature was a poem, that most marginal of artistic productions, and it was inscribed on a bronze tablet that now rests inside the statue's base. Here is the conclusion of "The New Colossus," by Emma Lazarus:

> *"Keep, ancient lands, your storied pomp!" cries she*
> *With silent lips. "Give me your tired, your poor,*
> *Your huddled masses yearning to breathe free,*
> *The wretched refuse of your teeming shore.*
> *Send these, the homeless, tempest-tost to me,*
> *I lift my lamp beside the golden door!"*

This is the sort of grand vision of liminality that the United States often calls forth. We are the threshold nation, the American self-myth says, offering doorway after doorway, behind each of which lies a new beginning.

This may be true, or nearly true. But there is a quieter, yet no less persistent, corollary: Those who pass through those doors will one day lift their own small light in a yellow wood, where two roads diverge. And it will make all the difference.

Acknowledgments

Ann Godoff, my editor, has been the truest friend and ally this book could have hoped for. I'm grateful in addition to the following people at Penguin Press: Benjamin Platt, Barbara Campo, Matt Boyd, Will Palmer, Sarah Hutson, Yamil Anglada, and Colin Dickerman (now at Flatiron Books).

Betsy Lerner, my agent, guides all of my writing that reaches book form. That's doubly true in this case, since this project was her inspiration.

Like anyone who writes on Robert Frost, I'm indebted to the scholars and Frost devotees who have spent decades tending the poet's legacy. Men work together, as the young Frost said, whether they work together or apart.

And I'm grateful as always to my family.

Further Reading
on Robert Frost and
"The Road Not Taken"

There are dozens of worthwhile books on Robert Frost. I've limited myself below to works that were particularly useful in this project and that I thought might appeal to general readers. I've necessarily excluded a number of admirable scholarly studies that are primarily engaged with other aspects of Frost (for instance, Robert Faggen's *Robert Frost and the Challenge of Darwin*), as well as some very fine books that are no longer in print (Reuben Brower's *The Poetry of Robert Frost: Constellations of Intention*).

WORK BY ROBERT FROST

Robert Frost: Collected Poems, Prose, and Plays, edited by Richard Poirier and Mark Richardson. This Library of America edition is the most reliable and comprehensive version of Frost's writing currently available. It includes everything but Frost's letters, so if you're looking for an all-encompassing Frost book, this is far and away the best option. It's only published in hardback, however, so for a paperback version of Frost's complete poetry, you'll have to go with the questionably edited

The Poetry of Robert Frost, prepared by Edward Lathem. (For the early poems, a better option is Robert Faggen's *Early Poems: Robert Frost*, which also includes a sampling from Frost's fourth book, *New Hampshire*.) For a paperback collection of Frost's prose, the best option is *The Collected Prose of Robert Frost*, edited by Mark Richardson.

The Letters of Robert Frost, Volume I (1886–1920), edited by Donald Sheehy, Mark Richardson, and Robert Faggen. This is the definitive edition of Frost's early letters. For the poet's later correspondence, there is as yet only the out-of-print and unreliable *Selected Letters*, compiled by Lawrance Thompson. (And to understand why the reliability of the edition matters, consider the following example that my copyeditor, Will Palmer, and I discovered in the letter to Louis Untermeyer discussed on pages 169 and 170 of this book. In that letter, Frost writes [emphasis mine], "There are no vampires there are no ghouls there are no demons, there is *no nothing* but me." In the *Selected Letters*, Thompson takes it upon himself to remove the "no" before "nothing," thereby changing the line to "there is nothing but me." It's a much less interesting formulation, and it isn't what Frost wrote.)

Elected Friends: Robert Frost & Edward Thomas to One Another, edited by Matthew Spencer. This volume gathers the correspondence between Frost and Thomas, allowing the reader to follow the intriguing progression of their friendship. Spencer also reproduces Thomas's early reviews of Frost, placing them chronologically among the letters. This material is bracketed by excellent critical essays by Michael Hofmann and Christopher Ricks.

BIOGRAPHIES OF FROST

Robert Frost: A Life by Jay Parini. A balanced and comprehensive biography aimed directly at general readers. Lawrance Thompson's three-volume behemoth can never be rivaled for sheer volume of information, but Parini's is by far the better, more readable book.

Frost: A Literary Life Reconsidered by William Pritchard. Half bi-
ography, half critique, this elegant study remains one of the finest intro-
ductions to Frost's life and work.

GENERAL READING AIDS

The Robert Frost Encyclopedia, edited by Nancy Lewis Tuten and John
Zubizarreta. An extraordinary resource that ranges across the entire
Frost enterprise. There are entries on all the individual poems, the
Frost biographical controversies, the Derry farm, almost everything
having to do with the poet.

Robert Frost Among His Poems by Jeffrey Cramer. Cramer's hugely
helpful book meticulously describes the literary and biographical con-
text in which individual poems were written. For example, "An Old
Man's Winter Night" "may have been inspired by Charles Lambert, a
local who lived for years as a hermit" in Derry.

The Art of Robert Frost by Tim Kendall. This unusual but invalu-
able book reproduces Frost's first four collections and a selection of
well-known later poems, supplementing every poem with a critical gloss
by Kendall. (In some cases, as with "The Road Not Taken," these
glosses run for two or three pages.) Kendall corrects a number of persis-
tent errors in his presentation of the text of the poems, and he's a pa-
tient, lively critic.

Robert Frost: The Work of Knowing by Richard Poirier. Poirier is
completely at ease with Frost's contradictions, and his examination of
the poet remains as crisp today as when it first appeared twenty-five
years ago. Readers up for a challenge may want to supplement Poirier's
book with Mark Richardson's *The Ordeal of Robert Frost*, which is
more overtly academic (it arose from Richardson's dissertation) but also
one of the most intelligent and sympathetic studies of the poet.

The Cambridge Companion to Robert Frost, edited by Robert Fag-
gen. A collection of fine scholarly essays on Frost by critics like William

Pritchard and Donald Sheehy. The more recent *Robert Frost in Context*, edited by Mark Richardson and also published by Cambridge University Press, supplements scholarly essays with criticism from poets like Paul Muldoon, as well as the perspective of Frost's granddaughter, Lesley Lee Francis.

INDEX

Titles are works by Frost unless otherwise noted.

INDEX

Printed in the United States
by Baker & Taylor Publisher Services